# Fly Fishing the Troutless River

Kevin App

Illustrations by Rosi Oldenburg

Kevin M. App
Newberg, OR 97132
Troutbum89@hotmail.com



Copyright © 2018 by Kevin App.

All rights reserved, including the right to reproduce this book or portions thereof in any form whatsoever. For information contact Kevin App.


Drawings Copyright © 2018 by Rosi Oldenburg.

All rights reserved.


Portions of this book have been previously published.

Library of Congress Control Number: 2018902057

ISBN 978-0-692-06302-6

# Contents

1  Tuesday Night                                                     1

2  Fade to Black                                                    16

3  The Iron Maidens                                                 26

4  Trout Wars: Return of the Angler                                 53

5  Don't Be So Negative                                             58

6  Born Again                                                       63

7  Suicide Weasels                                                  72

8  Fly Fishing the Troutless River                                 113

9  Cosmic Justice and Other Perils of Raising Fly Fishermen        128

10  "Winter" Steelheading                                          139

11  The First Fishing Guide                                        147

12  (Teeny) Footprints In the Sand                                 155

13  Night of the Grass-Popper                                      164

14  Cursed                                                         173

To my family; thank you all for putting up with my particular obsession for many years now; in particular my wife, who may not have known what she was getting into.

Special thanks to several folks who thought my stories were good enough to publish; Pat Hoglund (editor and publisher, *Salmon & Steelhead Journal*), who gave me my first chance in print; Nick Amato (editor, *Salmon Trout Steelheader*); Ben Romans (editor, *American Angler*), and Craig Schuhmann (editor, *Flyfishing & Tying Journal*).

Last but most certainly not least, thank you Rosi Oldenburg. Without your art, this whole project may not have ever been undertaken at all.

# Foreword

I am not a famous fly fisherman. I'm not a fly fishing "expert". I'm not a guide, I'm not a casting instructor. I'm not a celebrity or a retired professional athlete. I'm not a globe-trotting adventurer who can offer the reader a life lived vicariously. Oh, and just for the heck of it, I've also never been through a Master of Fine Arts program. In short, I'm just a regular guy, so who would care about my fishing stories?

Well, I didn't necessarily think anyone would when I started this project, or at least not many. It started out as the simple act of writing down some stories of past trips so that my kids (and future grandchildren) might have them to enjoy. That was sometime in late 2011. Though I have been a fan of "fly fishing literature" for many years, I didn't necessarily figure on publishing any of it.

My first attempts were somewhat dry, clumsy recountings of facts that even family members might have been less than likely to finish reading. The first thing I wrote was called *The Trip* (now known as *The Iron Maidens*). It's changed names more than once. It was the story of my first fly fishing trip, which led to this lifelong interest that I have, and so was particularly important.

The process was more challenging than I expected it to be. The story seemed too long, too heavy on details that a reader wouldn't be likely to care about. But I cared. I didn't want to drop the details. At the time I was watching my aging mother struggle with dementia, and perhaps I was a little worried that over time, it was the details that I would begin to forget myself. It seemed as though I was doomed to be unable to find a final form that I was happy with.

Rather than scrapping the whole idea I decided to shift gears, and try a shorter tale or two. I would use an approach intended to create stories similar to the ones I liked from books and magazines. I'd certainly read enough of them, so how hard could it be? The result was *Born Again*, the story of how I caught my first steelhead on a fly. Again, it was more difficult than I expected to get to a finished product, but I kept tinkering and refining until I had something that I was happy with.

I guess I must have been pretty happy with it at some point, because I started wondering if there was any chance of getting a story published in a fishing magazine. Everything I had heard on the topic suggested that my chances of success would be better if I tried out as a walk-on with the Mariners; but I was writing for fun at that point, and it couldn't hurt (too much, anyway) to try.

Without going into the gory details of multiple rejections, suffice it to say that it took some doing. About two years after I scribbled my first few words, I sold three stories to *Salmon & Steelhead Journal*. *Born Again* appeared in the October 2013 issue.

Since then I have continued writing, generally trying to keep the stories to a length and format so that they might work for a magazine. Many of the stories in this book have been previously published in *American Angler, Flyfishing & Tying Journal, Salmon Trout Steelheader,* and, of course *Salmon & Steelhead Journal*.

All of these stories are true. Perhaps someday I'll start embellishing some details for the sake of a more interesting tale, but so far I have not. A handful of stories remain that are too important to me personally to cut down to size for the sake of publication and packaging. *Tuesday Night* and *The Iron Maidens* explain how I came to my particular addiction, which I assume most of you share. *Suicide Weasels* is the story of my greatest fishing adventure (so far…). I couldn't bring myself to cut it down.

So, there you have it. Just a regular guy sharing some fishing stories. I have no grand illusions or lofty literary aspirations. The notion of writing the next *Walden* has never come to mind, or even the next *A River Never Sleeps*. I like humorous stories more than poignant or especially emotional ones, and so I try to make my stories funny when I can. The mishaps that seem to happen naturally in the wilderness help with that. I really just hope that the stories engage and entertain, and end up being relatable to a few fishermen out there.

Kevin App<br>
February, 2018

## Tuesday Night

I grew up near a river. It wasn't so close that I could stumble my way down to its' banks as a diaper-clad toddler, but by ten or eleven it was within biking range, and it quickly became our favorite destination for adolescent adventures. It was a great place to go exploring, and perfect for dirt-biking. One time we even had a make-shift paleontological dig (I dug up something that looked like the jaw-bone of some sort of horse; that counts as a fossil, dammit). Catching crawdads could be a good time, until we got carried away one day and came home with three hundred of the little suckers. We thought we could keep them alive by putting them in a bucket of water. I still feel bad about that. It was a straight-up Crawdaw Holocaust.

About the only thing we never did down by the river was fish. Maybe we would have if it had been possible, but I did not grow up near the junction of great trout streams; I grew up in suburban Southern California. The river near my childhood home was the Santa Ana River; and (at least in my neck of the woods), it was a concrete lined wash that often had no water in it (the crawdads lived in a little trickle of water that ran alongside the wash). Just a bit downhill from my hometown of Costa Mesa, it "flowed" through Huntington Beach on its' way to the Pacific Ocean, about three miles downstream. So, if you were thinking of drift boats, pine trees, and trout sipping mayflies, well, the reality looked more like the setting for the drag racing scene from *Grease,* or maybe the big chase sequence from *Terminator II*. No, I never fly fished as a child. In fact, I never fished at all, even though the ocean was just a few miles from our door. There was plenty for a kid to do though, so we never knew we were missing out on something.

All things considered, it seems odd that fly fishing became such an important part of my life. Very little would have had to happen differently for me to go through my entire life without ever picking up a rod. But let's not get ahead of ourselves. In fact, let's see if I can figure out how this all got started…

About a year after I graduated high school (that would make it 1990) my brother Chris and I were sharing an apartment in Costa Mesa. For those who have no idea where that is, it sits just inland of Newport Beach; and since most everyone knows where that is, I used to explain my hometown by telling people that if your feet aren't actually in sand, then you're probably in Costa Mesa rather than Newport Beach.

My oldest friend Clayton Nelson was still in town as well. Without intending to put too fine a point on it, we were bored. We all had college and part time jobs to keep us busy, that wasn't the problem. Not that there's anything new or different about young men being restless and longing for adventure, but I don't think we had yet realized that that was what was going on, or how to find worthwhile outlets for our wanderlust. If someone had told me back then that fishing was just what I needed, well let's just say I probably wouldn't have taken them seriously.

It just so happened that we all had Tuesday nights off, and so the ritual of getting together on Tuesdays was born. It started out simply enough; killing time around our apartment watching old episodes of Star Trek and trying to decide what to do. I guess that still strikes me as odd, since none of us were "Trekkies" by any stretch of the imagination. I never liked the show as a kid, but for some reason we decided as young men that Kirk, Bones, and Spock were funny as all get out. I'm sure beer hand a hand in that, but anyway we would eventually decide on some place to grab a bite to eat and then find the nearest place to shoot a few games of pool before calling it a night. It wasn't exactly a life of adventure.

After a few weeks of the same routine we were sitting in my apartment one Tuesday night trying to figure out where to go to eat. The usual place was Wahoo's Fish Taco, a little place around the corner that was made out to look like a surfer's beach hut and served food that was, well, hard to categorize. The called it a fusion of Brazilian, Asian, and Mexican. Whatever you want to call it, we liked it, and it had become our most common haunt; but Clay had something else in mind that night.

"Let's go to Ye Olde King's Head." Clay suggested.

Ye Olde King's Head was a British pub and restaurant near the beach in Santa Monica. As British pubs go, it felt like a pretty authentic place. We used to joke that the only ones there on any given night (besides ourselves) who didn't sound like honest-to-God Englishmen were the Australians. We'd discovered the place the year before, and we'd had a good time trying to finish off "king size" orders of fish and chips (which consisted of two pieces of battered, deep-fried fish, each approximately the size of a regulation NFL football, along with a side of fries) while sitting under a portrait of Winston Churchill. The catch was that it was over fifty miles away and it would take an hour or so to get there, assuming we didn't hit traffic (never a given in So Cal). None of us had been driving for more than a few years, and a road trip for no practical reason wasn't something that we did. Well, not until that night anyway.

"Are you serious?" I replied, figuring he wasn't.

"Let's go, Bro. Get off your butt." Clay said, somehow sensing he was onto something.

Between where we were sitting and Santa Monica there had to be a million places to eat. There was no logical reason to drive into L.A. just for fish and chips. Suddenly that seemed appealing.

"Okay, let's go" I answered.

Of course we went and had a good time. We got home way too late and made sure to vow not to be so stupid next week; but when the next Tuesday came, it was a different tune. Once again we were sitting around my old apartment trying to decide where to go to eat. We were aware that we all had things to do the next morning, and last week's adventure had been paid for in exhaustion the next day. Still, beneath the tone of responsibility that we were trying to maintain there was a palpable desire in the room to one-up our previous week's effort. As we were kicking around names of pricey seafood joints in Newport Beach without any real enthusiasm for the idea, Clay lobbed the next grenade into mix:

"Let's go to Big Bear." He stated as if it was just around the corner.

Big Bear meant a little town near Big Bear Lake in the San Bernardino National Forest. It was a popular area to visit among skiers since it was only one hundred miles away; a two hour drive to the east. Clay had been there a number of times. Chris and I weren't skiers and had never been, but we still knew it was a very long way to go for dinner.

"Are you serious?" I asked in a moment of déjà vu.

"We're going." Clay replied as if my question had sealed the matter.

The three of us made the two hour drive. Starting at our apartment just a mile or so from the beach in southern California, we drove until we were in the snow covered mountains of ski country. In addition to the silliness of driving so far without actually knowing if we would find a place to eat when we got there, we had also gotten a late start, and ended up rolling into Big Bear around eleven, and were nigh on starving by then. The only place we found open was a little hole-in-the-wall that was called (at the time anyway) Joe's Alpine Café.

Maybe the kitchen staff, who were probably thinking they were just about done for the night, were a little confused when the order came in for six dinners for our party of three, but I must say that both the fried chicken and the prime rib were surprisingly good. And we put it away like Shaggy and Scooby on a good day, if I do say so myself.

We got home after two in the morning, and we all had class the next day, and so the parts of ourselves that were attempting to bloom into responsible adults probably experienced some regret, once again. But another part experienced something of an epiphany, whether we realized it at the time or not. There was something inherently satisfying about going way farther than necessary for no particular reason.

We would end up discussing how we were going to top the trip to Big Bear in subsequent weeks. Someone brought up San Francisco, but that would have required plane tickets. We either weren't so crazy as to hop on a plane to San Francisco for no better reason than to get dinner and fly home the same night, or we were just too broke to even consider such a thing. It appeared that we had limited out on what a group of broke college students could do to turn a weeknight dinner into a makeshift adventure. Maybe that's why our little tradition faded away, or maybe it was just because peoples' schedules changed, or some such thing. It wasn't all that long before Clay moved out to Tucson to finish school at the University of Arizona. But the seed had been planted.

Fast forward a few years to 1993. We were all now living in Tucson and attending the University of Arizona. By that time I had been out fishing a few times and was starting to really get into the idea. I hadn't yet picked up a fly rod; that would come later in the year. It was June, and Clay and I were talking about taking a quick trip to the White Mountains to get in a little early season trout fishing, and some camping as well. We both had three days available. To maximize our fishing time we were planning to leave for our trip after I got off of work and drive at night. That would be a pretty aggressive effort, seeing as how I was working at a fine dining restaurant and typically got off of work late. With a four hour drive to our destination, we could easily be looking at arriving in the early morning hours and getting only a little or maybe even no sleep at all.

As the time for our trip approached, perhaps a week away, I got a call from Clay.

"I was thinking that we should just go to Lee's Ferry." Clay suggested.

"How far away is that?" I asked, having never been there.

"It's about a six and a half hour drive; four hundred miles. The fishing will be worth it." Clay assured me.

"This sounds kind of crazy; kind of stupid, too. Okay, let's do it." I answered.

This was beginning to sound like a suicide mission, but the fishing at Lee's Ferry was supposed to be fantastic. All we had to do was get through the drive the first night and then it would be a couple of days of nothing but fishing and relaxing beside a camp fire. We made all of our preparations over the next few days, then, only a day before our trip was to begin, I got another phone call.

"Let's go to Colorado." Said Clay, as if it was no big deal.

"Are you serious?" I asked.

The words hung in the air for a moment, bringing to mind our Tuesday night adventures from a couple of years earlier. Somehow we both understood that this response meant that we had to do whatever had been suggested, regardless of how ridiculous the suggestion might be.

"Let's go fish the San Miguel. You're going to love this place, Dealer." Clay offered, trying to convince me that it was a good idea, but knowing that it didn't really matter.

The nickname "Dealer", in case you were wondering, was one that went back to our high school days, and any one of our little group might be likely to use it on any other. Rest assured, it had nothing to do with drugs. Anyway, the San Miguel was a small stream near Telluride that Clay had fished on a two week trip through the Rocky Mountains the year before with his former dorm-mate, Jeff Garza. It was six hundred miles away. If we drove straight through without stopping it would take us ten and a half hours. This was just plain nuts, and there was no way it could possibly be worth it.

"All right, I'm in." I responded, as I was obligated to at that point. "Of course you realize that we'll probably die trying to pull this off..." I added.

"We can do this, Dealer."

There was still time to adjust our plan. We didn't have the internet, of course, so Clay went down to Triple A and got a trip-tick, which detailed the fastest route. The day of the trip arrived, and I touched base with Clay before heading off to work that afternoon. The brain fever hadn't passed, he still wanted to go to Colorado, and we were all set.

As luck would have it, it was not an early night. It was busy at the restaurant, which meant that I had a roll of cash in my pocket to cover expenses, but it was one in the morning before we got on the road. I can't remember how much discussion there was about coming to our senses, but either way, we didn't. We headed north, putting our faith in strong coffee and Metallica.

Our journey took us past Lee's Ferry, and we also blew right past the San Juan River.

"I've heard that there are trout in there." Clay mentioned as we crossed the San Juan around the four corners region.

We might as well have been crossing over the Santa Ana for all of the attention we gave to one of the Southwest's greatest trout streams.

"Cool. By the way, can you see dancing babies on the road ahead?" I replied.

"No... can't say that I do. No dancing babies."

"I figured it was just me. Since I'm hallucinating, you should probably take over driving."

It was afternoon of the next day by the time we were nearing our destination. At the very least, the scenery didn't disappoint. It was exactly how a kid from California expected Colorado to look; mountain peaks so high and jagged they didn't seem quite real, with plenty of snow clinging to the tallest; and forests of evergreens and aspens in every direction.

We rolled into Clay's secret camping spot on the river exhausted, but in good spirits. We had made it, and now we would have our reward.

There was a wall of heavy brush between us and the river and the first thing I wanted to do was to get a look at the water. I walked down to the stream while Clay began to unload the truck. It was June in the high country of Colorado. The newly warm weather was having a predictable effect on the local rivers; one that we, as total neophytes, had not considered.

"We have a problem." I said as I walked back into the camp site. "It's chocolate milk down there, and it's running hard."

"You're kidding." Clay responded.

We walked back down to the river and stared for a few minutes.

"Maybe it's still fishable..." Someone offered, knowing it wasn't.

"I think we're out of luck."

There was nothing we could do. The San Miguel was unfishable. Trying to wade the normally small river would result in being quickly swept downstream by the high, muddy flow. We had no choice but to do the one thing we should have done before embarking on this little quest; we had to ask someone for advice. We got back on the road and went looking for any place we could find that looked like there might be someone inside who could point us toward a body of water that held fish. When we finally found such a place the answer we got was predictable.

"Every river around here is going to be blown out. You could try some of the lakes. There is a nice little spot not too far away that you can fish from shore and camp where there probably won't be anyone else around. It's called Beaver Lake." The store clerk told us.

We got directions and thanked him for his help. It was late afternoon by then, but we were determined to find a spot and catch some fish before it got dark. That was all we had left. It would be a long night in camp with nothing to think about except our own stupidity otherwise.

We found the rather ingloriously named Beaver Lake and set up camp as quickly as we could. In our haste to get set up and get to fishing, I didn't immediately notice what a pretty little spot it was; nicely secluded, uncrowded, and with one hell of a view. The campground was set in among a patch of spruce trees, and the lake was surrounded by a small meadow, with the mountains of the Uncompahgre National Forest in the background. The sounds of the Cimarron River flowing nearby completed the package, though we didn't try to fish it.

It was just starting to get dark as we walked down to the lake to try to get a few trout for dinner. We had left at one in the morning the previous night, and here we were just starting to fish as the sun was going down. Clay and I began working the shoreline, moving in opposite directions, hoping to put casts in front of as many fish as possible. Clay had an old fly rod that he got from his grandfather, I was using the only fishing rod I owned at the time, a cheap medium-action spinning rod and reel that I used for everything. I was casting lures, primarily my old standby, the Mepps Aglia Gold.

Rings of rising trout disturbed the otherwise calm surface of the lake as dusk descended. I launched my lure out into the thick of things and retrieved it back, hoping for a tug. Again, then again, and then came a good solid grab. I reared back on it like I was setting a 5/0 hook on a fifteen pound largemouth, then reeled it in as quickly as I could. No time to enjoy the battle, or even, it seemed, to pay much attention to the fish. Uncermoniously wacking my prize over the head, I tossed him in some grass next to me and went back to fishing as quickly as I could. We needed several to make dinner for two.

Night fell within a half hour and I saw Clay walking back toward me as the last light faded. He had walked all the way around to the other side of the small lake. He wasn't carrying any fish.

"Did you get anything?" He asked as he walked up.

"Just one." I responded, pointing to the trout lying in the grass.

"Bro, that thing is a mackerel! That'll feed both of us!" Clay exclaimed.

I glanced down at the silver-sided fish lying still in the grass beside me. In my short fishing career I had yet to catch anything more substantial than a pan-sized stocker. Could it be that I had landed a personal best without noticing? So it was. Chrome-colored and plump, it ran around twenty inches, and it did indeed feed us both.

It was a clear, starry night, and the air at just under 9,000 feet in elevation was cold; cold in a way that a kid from the beaches of Southern California couldn't reconcile with the beginning of summer. I guess it was lucky for me in the end, because when I managed to bump my forearm against the iron rim of the camp fire pit (while the fire was going) and sear a nice little scar into my flesh, the chilly night air soothed it quickly. I didn't really even mind, as I had no cool scars at the time, and that one ended up being something of a souvenir of the trip. It took four or five years to fade out completely, and I could tell the story of how I got it so that it sounded a bit like Kwai Chang Caine burning little dragons into his forearms at the Shaolin Monastery. My scar actually looked kind of like a dragon, except without wings, claws, fangs, or arms and legs. Okay, it looked like a slug, but there's a college in California that actually chose a slug as its mascot. That has to count for something.

I suppose we could have spent the evening dwelling on the silliness of the whole undertaking. After all, we could have fished a stocked pond a whole lot closer to home. Somehow we didn't see it that way, or even if we did, it wasn't a negative. We were in Colorado, camping in the Rocky Mountains! The fact that we had driven there on a weeknight after work, virtually on a whim, made it *better*. I'm not sure how many times we looked at each other and said: "Dude, we're in Colorado", and then proceeded to clink our bottles in a toast to our accomplishment (I guess you can tell at this point I hadn't traveled much as a young person), but it was more than once.

Besides, I'd caught my first Rocky Mountain trout, and it was a dandy. We sautéed it in butter with some bacon and green onions, and it still stands out in memory as one of the best trout dinners I have ever had. A little thing like driving all night to catch a single fish wasn't going to ruin it for me.

My first effort at casting a fly rod came that weekend as well. We were fishing Silver Jack Reservoir, just down the road from our camp site, and Clay handed me his rod and asked if I wanted to give it a shot. The clouds parted, a light shone down from Heaven, and the sound of angles singing rose over the mountaintops as I took the rod. I managed something that approximated a back-cast, meaning that the line was somewhere behind me, though I'm sure it neither straightened out properly nor was it in-line for an accurate (or particularly safe) forward cast. Nevertheless, I was set up well enough to bring my rod forward and get that line moving with some authority. I waited for an excruciatingly long split-second for the line to unfurl perfectly and drop the dry fly on the water so daintily that nothing with fins could possibly resist rising to consume it. Instead I heard a sharp *whack* and felt something slam into the back of my head. The line stopped short, falling in a heap around me. Isn't there a saying about great endeavors and humble beginnings? At least I was wearing a hat, which now was decorated with its' first fly.

We found only modest fishing success for the rest of the weekend. I guess it didn't bother us too much. We were still beginners, and weren't exactly accustomed to catching loads of fish. The camping was fun, the scenery was great, and it was just cool being in Colorado for the first time. But with or without a cooler full of trout, the time came to begin the trek home.

This was, of course, another opportunity for wandering, and being unwilling to let it go by without taking full advantage, we decided to take a different route home. We would go through Durango, where we were sure to find someplace interesting to eat at the very least.

Durango has a distinctively different feel from most other ski towns in Colorado. For starters, it isn't so much in the mountains as it is at the base of them. At 6,500 feet above sea level, it's only a bit higher up than Denver. In case you're wondering, that means it's still high desert, and the feel of the place is more like a quaint little western town than a mountain ski town; or perhaps the best way to describe it is a sort of fusion of the two. However one chooses to describe it, it works.

Starting in a part of town that looked promising, we wandered on foot for a while without finding what we were looking for. High priced tourist traps abounded, and were we not broke college students that might have worked, but it wasn't what we were hoping for. Just when it looked like we would be settling for Big Macs and fries, something unexpected happened.

"App!" A voice called loudly from somewhere.

We both stopped short, alternately looking at each other with puzzled expressions and looking around in hopes of figuring out where the voice had come from. I wasn't aware of anyone I knew who lived in Durango.

"App!" The voice called again.

This time I located the source of the voice. It was coming from across the street, where someone was standing in front of a little ski shop. From where I was standing all I could tell was that the person who had identified me on the streets of a little ski town in a sparsely populated corner of a state that I had never visited before was around five and a half feet tall, and despite having the kind of pattern baldness one normally associates with middle-age, gave the distinct impression of someone around my age, in other words early twenties.

"I have no idea of who that is. How about you?" I asked Clay.

"Not a clue." He answered.

When we got close enough we both recognized the guy, who we knew from the baseball team back at Estancia High, and things suddenly made a bit more sense. His name was Shawn Bouley, and he had been a couple of years behind us in school. We didn't really know each other well, but apparently well enough that he recognized me on the streets of Durango. He was there going to school (and skiing). I seemed to remember that his hair had been a little thin on top even as a high school sophomore, so even that part now made sense. Of course, he turned out to be the perfect source of information on interesting "locals" places to eat.

Maybe you have to be a bit of a "foodie" to think finding the perfect place for beers and burgers is so important. If so, then, guilty as charged. Hey, I worked my way through college in fine dining rooms, so sue me. Anyway, some places just make an impression; the kind of impression that keeps you from ever going through their neck of the woods again without stopping in. Olde Tymers Café, located in an old brick building with the painted signs of its previous life as a "druggist" still visible on the walls, eclectic decoration, great burgers, and a dark lager on tap from Durango Brewing Company is just such a place. Hell, I could go for a burger and a Durango Dark right now.

I never saw Shawn Bouley again, so I never got to thank him. If you ever stumble across this story Shawn; thanks, I owe you one.

The rest of the trip home was uneventful, or so we thought at the time. We made one stop in Shiprock, New Mexico, to get gas and some road snacks. Shiprock is a small town on the Navajo Reservation in the four corners area, where Arizona, Colorado, New Mexico, and Utah connect. Getting the rest of the way home proved to be challenging, as exhaustion was quickly catching up with us. We had been operating on adrenaline for several days. Starting with a sleepless night, we had proceeded to stay up late around the fire, then fish from dawn till dark the next day, and then stay up late around the fire again. In addition to sleep deprivation, we were both showing cold symptoms by the time we got home. Neither of us thought too much of it; we had pushed ourselves a bit too hard and it looked like we were going to have to pay the piper, nothing more. We managed to make it back to Tucson, and I walked into my apartment and immediately collapsed into bed, believing the adventure was at its' end.

First thing the next morning I got a call from Clay. He had heard from his very concerned mother that there was an outbreak of a mysterious virus around the four corners Navajo Reservation. Several people had died. They couldn't figure out what it was, but it started out with cold symptoms and progressed from there to respiratory failure. Neither of us thought there was much chance we could have contracted whatever it was just by stopping at a gas station, but we both clearly had colds, so we weren't completely unconcerned either.

"What a way for us to go out; whacked by a virus." Clay said as we contemplated the very slim, but still possible chance that we both had some unidentifiable killer disease.

"If we were going to die we could have at least caught a few more fish…" I added.

Before too long the sickness was identified as Hantavirus, spread through rodent droppings. A dozen people had died as a result of it by then. Based on what we heard about how it was spread, we didn't think there was any way we could have been exposed, but neither of us really rested easy until the colds cleared up.

All in all it had been a pretty silly thing to do, even without the whole Hantavirus incident. One couldn't possibly make a logical argument that it had been worth it to put in thirty-plus hours of driving over the course of three days to catch the few fish we managed to get. On top of it all we'd gone right past several great fisheries only to end up at a little lake filled with stocked trout. Somehow we were still pretty satisfied with ourselves. Sure we wished we had caught more fish, or bigger fish, or both; but whether we truly realized it at the time or not, that was never really the point.

Maybe it takes early twenty-something men to properly appreciate going way farther than you need to go just for its' own sake. As the metaphysical descendant of our old Tuesday night adventures it represented the pinnacle of pointless wanderlust. But then, perhaps not pointless after all. It was my first exposure to the Rocky Mountains. They were just one (ridiculously long) day's drive away. The possibilities were endless, especially if one were to actually think ahead and make a rational plan; you know, everything we hadn't done on this trip. Oh well, you have to start somewhere, even if it's a humble little spot called Beaver Lake.

## Fade to Black

  The mid-day sun was high overhead as we pulled away from the marina at Roosevelt Lake. The heat of the Arizona summer was relentless, and the three of us were sweat-soaked and a couple of shades darker than we were when we arrived the previous afternoon. The feeling in the cab of that old truck was at least as much shell-shock and disbelief as it was frustration. We cranked up the air conditioner and the stereo, throwing in the only thing that would capture the mood just right. It was common for us to listen to that song at the end of a fishing trip, but after what we'd just experienced, it seemed more appropriate than ever. The first blasts of cool air began as the familiar sound of a single acoustic guitar filled the cab. It was going to be a long drive home.

  I still think of that trip any time I hear that song, even after more than twenty years, but that's hardly unique. Music and road trips (and fishing trips) just go together; so it's only natural that some of them just bring back the memories. Any time I hear *That Summer* by Garth Brooks I can't help thinking of my first fly fishing trip to the San Juan River in 1993. Sure, that song has nothing to do with fishing, and the lyrics are even a bit disturbing if you stop and think about them. Before you let your mind wander into the gutter, I did not have an illicit affair with an older woman while on that trip. The song just happened to be playing on the radio as I caught my first glimpse of the river canyon at sunrise.

Strange pairings like that are far from unusual. In fact, that seems to be the norm, particularly if you tend to listen to the radio when you're out in the boonies, as I generally do. Throw in a DJ who's determined to play a particular song fifty times in a day and things can get really bizarre; like remembering a fall steelheading trip on the Grande Ronde whenever you hear *Our Song* by Taylor Swift; which may or may not be weirder than thinking of fly fishing the San Juan when you hear a song about a teenage virgin schtupping a horny widow.

Speaking of weird, I once spent a day swinging flies for winter steelhead on the East Fork of the Lewis River with songs from my daughter's *"Toddler Tunes"* CD stuck in my head no matter how hard I tried to purge them. I'm pretty sure I was timing my casts to the tune of *Bobby Shafto's Gone to Sea*. Of course I got skunked that day. The fish knew. I had a coach in high school who believed that a baseball had such psychic powers (his favorite expression was "the ball knows"), so why not a steelhead? That's as good an excuse as any for not catching fish; keeping in mind that Coach was something of a character, who refused to accept the notion that a football was a ball at all (it isn't round) and instead referred to it as a meatloaf.

Anyway, this whole phenomenon seems to happen completely randomly; or at least that's been my experience. Whether it's some song on the radio that has nothing to do with anything, or a tune that's stuck in my head against my will, I generally have no choice in the matter, and I can't seem to force it, with only the rarest of exceptions. That day at Roosevelt Lake was one of those exceptions. The music was chosen to match the moment, and the memory stuck. But I'm getting ahead of myself. Let's start from the beginning.

We did a lot of bass fishing back in the day. By that I mean the early 1990s, when I was a student at the University of Arizona. I was new to the sport, as were most of the members of our little band of merry men. With no parental benefactor to offer a boat and a lifetime of experience to share, we were left to figure things out on our own. It sure seemed like we spent most of our time paying our dues the hard way.

Our lack of experience was complimented by a lack of equipment. The whole "broke college student" thing puts certain natural limitations on one's arsenal of gear. None of us had a boat, and we didn't have specialized rods for every species of fish. Perhaps that might sound strange based on what you see in today's fly fishing media, where you can find images of early twenty-somethings, complete with long hair and facial stubble, wearing $800 waders and carrying a $1000 rod paired with a $600 reel, excitedly hopping off a chartered helicopter in some remote wilderness location to fish a river that has never even been seen by another human being before. While I'm sure this helps to create a hip, young image for the sport, that's not quite the way I remember life as a young angler. But then I suppose even Brad Pitt wouldn't look good in rubber chest waders, so I won't be holding my breath to see anglers in cheap gear adorning the covers of fly fishing magazines.

So, we had to find bass lakes that could be fished effectively from shore. That's how we ended up at Roosevelt Lake, which wasn't particularly close to Tucson, but had good shore access, along with a marina for the times when we could scrape together the cash for a rental.

Located about 80 miles northeast of Phoenix, the 33.5 square-mile lake lies between distinctively southwestern mountain ranges. Here you won't find slopes adorned with pine forests, but rather low-lying brush and multiple species of cactus. The iconic Saguaro grows in abundance here, and stands like a sentinel above the rest of the landscape. Multi-colored layers of rock jut from the hillsides to complete the effect.

The Sonoran desert leaves few who experience it unmoved, but how one reacts is often a question of perspective. It is a place of stark natural beauty; easily appreciated when viewed on a postcard, or even from an air-conditioned vehicle. It is also unavoidably harsh; a place where even the plants are armed for battle, and dried bones beckon the unwary to join them; which is generally the side you notice when hiking through it at high noon on a summer day. Either way, sticking around until sunset can get you front row seats for the most spectacular display of colors this side of the Aurora Borealis.

The lake has good populations of both largemouth and smallmouth bass. We usually focused on smallmouth, after finding a huge rock-pile that attracted them like packs of unsupervised teenagers in the woods draw invincible, supernatural psycho-killers. We could walk out onto the sharp, less-than-stable rocks, but not a single step could be taken without care. Of course, we did this with our hands full of fishing gear and probably a cooler that was large enough to be hard to manage. That meant that there really wasn't any catching yourself in the event of a slip, unless you consider smashing your butt or your knee rather than your head to be "catching yourself". None of us ever went for x-rays to confirm, but we were pretty sure that those shifting rocks were responsible for at least one broken tailbone, if not several. What can I say? That was where the fish were…

The Sonoran Desert is also home to a myriad of infamous critters, and fishing on foot means keeping an eye out for rattlesnakes, tarantulas, Gila monsters, scorpions, etc. With all of those choices, I guess we never expected to end up in a Mexican stand-off with a battalion of skunks. Apparently they considered our rock-pile part of their turf, and they were unwilling to give it up. Rather than scurrying away when we approached, they stood their ground. Several warning shots with rocks large enough to crush them had no effect. They actually seemed to prefer death to retreat. I had no idea that skunks were so valiant; like little foul-smelling wolverines.

I don't know; perhaps God gave skunks their formidable defensive capabilities because they are actually too stupid to survive, and would quickly go extinct otherwise. Or maybe you just get cocky when you're the size of a house cat and can chase off a bear. Either way, there was something about their defiant, unyielding stand. It was like they were taunting us; daring us to kill one of them and see what happened. You could almost hear the last words of Obi-Wan Kenobi in their icy stare… "You can't win. If you strike me down, I shall become more powerful than you can possibly imagine."

When we weren't too busy battling skunks or breaking supposedly vestigial body parts, we would spend our days baking in the sun as we plied the water with our assortment of artificial aquatic life forms. A particularly hot day (and there were a few of them) could mean a very real danger of dehydration. Each man virtually needed his own personal water tower, and under-estimating your water needs would bring your day to a premature end; which was, of course, better than staying out in one hundred twenty degree heat without water and bringing your life to a premature end. It wasn't common for us to sound the general retreat in the middle of a fishing day for fear of imminent death, but it did happen.

It probably sounds like we had all stepped well across the (sometimes) thin line separating fishermen from masochists. Maybe so, but it wasn't all suffering and brushes with death. The productive days were enough to keep us coming back, despite the challenges. Still, when you suffer for every fish you can't help thinking about finding a better way. There were rumors of great bass fishing going on in our favorite lakes at night, and it made sense to us. After all, daytime highs were well over one hundred degrees. A twenty-four hour boat rental from the marina at Roosevelt Lake seemed like the perfect plan; we could fish all night long and finally get our share. No skunks (they don't swim after you, do they?), no rocks, no broken tailbones.

So it was that the three of us, my old friend Clayton Nelson, my brother Chris, and I all piled into Clay's little two-door Nissan truck and headed off to Roosevelt Lake. We planned to get our boat in the afternoon and get ourselves to some good water while it was light out, stake out a fishy spot, and clobber 'em all night.

The afternoon began with high hopes. We sped across the lake in our little rented boat, the breeze off the water offering some relief from the last of the day's heat. Okay, the rental was sporting a twenty-five horsepower outboard, so perhaps "sped" is a bit of an exaggeration. We were moving anyway. Add that to the road trip from Tucson, and we'd put in four hours by the time we reached Goose Flats; a part of the lake that was rumored to be kicking out lots of fish. No matter, our efforts were about to pay off big-time. It was early evening, as planned; the sun low in the sky, the heat finally losing some of its' sting.

There were a number of other boats around, but they appeared to be packing it in. One of the others motored up beside us as we were getting set up to fish.

"Man, you guys just missed it. They were lighting it up on top in here just a few minutes ago, but then it just died." The guy driving the boat told us.

"You're kidding, right?" One of us offered.

"Nope. It was rockin' in here. I'm not sure why it died off so suddenly, but it's time for me to call it a day. I hope you guys have some luck." He said as he started off toward the marina.

We stood there staring at each other, exchanging looks of horror and disbelief. Just what sort of clichés-gone-awry alternate universe had we wandered into? As a fisherman, you expect to hear "You should have been here yesterday" sometimes, or even "You should have been here last week". Only in the Ninth Plane of Hell would someone say "You should have been here five seconds ago" and actually mean it. Had we done something to call the wrath of Murphy down on ourselves? Could it be that we had come all of this way only to miss our chance by mere minutes? No, that couldn't be true. There were fish in there, and we had all night to get 'em.

The sun went down in an explosion of red, orange, and purple as we made cast after cast in search of a fish or two still willing to bite; not that we paid much attention to the scenery in our frenzied attempts to induce a strike from the fish, which had clearly all spontaneously disintegrated.

Darkness fell and the temperature began to drop. We hadn't neglected to prepare for this, and even managed to change into jeans and sweatshirts without capsizing the small boat.

We kept at it for hours; trying one thing after another, casting blindly into the darkness, hoping for the tug of a fish to break up the monotony. Meanwhile the stars came out, innumerable in the perfectly clear night sky… and the Earth's warmth was quickly sucked out into space.

Young men are notorious for believing themselves to be invincible, so being impervious to the elements should be a relatively minor thing. God knows all children believe that they can play outside in a blizzard in nothing but their underwear with no problem. All of mine have certainly suffered from this particular delusion. The youngest had such a disdain for wearing any clothing at all for the first several years of her life that we considered purchasing a home in a nudist colony to prevent shocking the neighbors. At what age this effect fully wears off is unclear. I've heard that the latest research shows that the brain isn't fully developed until about age twenty-four, which begs the question of whether we might want to take another look at the legal voting age.

Anyway, as midnight approached we had caught two fish between the three of us, the wind was blowing, and it was getting really cold. At some point, spending the night in the truck actually sounded better than shivering and shaking for six more fishless hours.

It was not our proudest moment. The whole point of the trip was to fish through the night. Speeding back across the lake only served to magnify the wind chill factor, and we were ready to stuff ourselves into a sardine can by the time we made it back to the marina, so long as it was warm. Of course the place was locked up, so we had to jump the fence to get back to the truck. Three grown men in the cab of a small truck is a bit crowded for driving to the corner store, to say nothing of a three hour road-trip. Trying to sleep that way is pretty well impossible.

We emerged from our metal cocoon before the sun came up the next morning, as much a result of the pointlessness of continuing to try to sleep as of our motivation to fish. There was still time to redeem ourselves. It wouldn't get really hot for a few hours, so we had a decent chance of finding willing fish.

Figuring that there was at least one spot that we knew would hold fish, we made our way over to our favorite smallmouth hole. We arrived just as the sky began to lighten with the approach of dawn. Finally, we would get to fish that spot without having to contend with those (@$%&!!) rocks.

We cruised slowly through the glassy waster as dawn broke, the whole world silent aside from the soft humming of the motor and the occasional bird chirping with the arrival of the new day.

"Oh (&%@!!$)!"

Clay's shout broke the spell, and before I knew what was happening, he'd jumped to his feet, killed the motor, and jerked it out of the water.

"Look down." He said in response to the puzzled stares he was getting from Chris and me.

I gazed into the water just as we floated over a mountain of rocks that nearly broke the surface. (#&*?%$!) rocks.

The rest of the morning passed slowly as we tried one spot after another. The fish were no more interested in our offerings than they had been the night before. By the time afternoon came and it was time to head back in, we had only picked up one more fish. We were tired, hungry, and defeated. We had been frozen, thawed out, and finally roasted in the Arizona summer heat. Three fish had been caught between three people over the course of a twenty-four hour trip. Back at the marina we turned in the boat and settled up with the clerk. He had a story to tell.

There was a guy who spent the day fishing for crappie off the dock with an ultralight rod loaded with four pound test. He hooked something big several times, but each time it broke his line. The fish kept coming back, and finally he lucked out and was able to land it. It turned out to be a fourteen pound largemouth, which would be in the ballpark of a record for the lake. As I recall the clerk said that they were going to get the fish back or perhaps a replica for their wall.

Once again we were left staring at each other, shaking our heads in disbelief. Had we not suffered for the sake of fish? Shouldn't we have been first in line for a little good fish-karma? Apparently not. It was the guy who just walked down to the dock and sat on his butt with an ultralight for a few hours. We covered a zillion square miles of water and the biggest fish in the whole damn lake was right beneath the dock at the marina.

As we walked back to the truck, the comments were predictable.

"I (#*@!!%) quit." Clay said.

Chris concurred: "Never fishing again…"

"I'm breaking all of my rods." I added.

And so there was no question as to what was going in the cassette deck as we pulled away from the marina; and to this day, any time I hear Metallica's *Fade to Black* I'm back in that little truck, crammed in with my brother and Clay, driving home after our most humiliating defeat since we first picked up a rod and reel.

I'm not sure if the fish that guy caught from the dock made it onto the wall at the Roosevelt Lake Marina, but apparently there is an old fish mount there now, more than twenty years later, of a largemouth bass in the twelve to fifteen pound range. It's been there so long that no one seems to know the story behind it. If you're ever out there check it out. Maybe it's the same fish, maybe not. I prefer to believe that it is. If so, then now you know, as Paul Harvey would say, the rest of the story.

## The Iron Maidens

I picked up fly fishing while in college. Yes, I know that's not a unique story, or even an unusual one. I've heard many versions of the same tale, generally set at someplace like the University of Montana; where one could while away the hours between classes on the trout stream that (all but) ran right through campus, pondering Plato and Aristotle while casting dry flies to rising trout.

I was a few clicks south of that, at the University of Arizona. About the only thing that I could have convinced to take a dry fly in Tucson would have been the bats that used to flap around outside of my apartment balcony every night at dusk. I could flip pennies in their direction and they would chase them, so why not an artificial fly?

I suppose the thought of what I might do if I actually managed to hook a bat kept me from trying it. But let's not get too far ahead of ourselves. I hadn't come to Tucson looking for fish; in fact, the thought never even crossed my mind.

I didn't hunt or fish as a child, but growing up in southern California (in the seventies and eighties) I never felt deprived. The weather was good enough to play our favorite sports twelve months a year, and that was just what we did. The beach was within biking distance; and Disneyland and Knott's Berry Farm were just down the road as well. What more could a kid ask for?

We spent most of our time on sports, but I didn't just see my favorite sports merely as a fun way to pass the time. They captured my imagination. I knew all the players on all the teams and an astounding array of statistics. That was the norm at the time, of course, and most of my childhood friends were the same. But the games also had a story to tell; at least for those who were interested. Old time greats and the games the way they were in their early years fascinated me. So while all of my friends knew Roger Staubach and Terry Bradshaw (and you would have been likely to find me on any given day sporting a jersey with number twelve in either white and blue or black and yellow), and any one of them probably could've quoted you Rod Carew's batting average on demand, only my twin brother Chris or I could have told you the story of how Sammy Baugh (quarterback for the Washington Redskins circa 1937 – 1952) once knocked an opposing player out cold by firing a bullet pass and hitting him right between the eyes as payback for a couple of particularly nasty sacks in a pre-facemask era game. That was the space I had to fill in my life when I grew up and had to leave (playing) organized sports behind.

I ended up at the University of Arizona somewhat by accident. When you grow up in California, it can be pretty easy to believe that you live in the center of the universe, so why would you want to leave? People were supposed to want to move *to* California, not *away* from it…

Well, I guess my thinking changed some by the time I had been out of high school for a year or so. The first inklings of wanderlust had begun to kick in, and some new scenery started to sound good. A couple of close friends had gone out to Arizona for school and they helped convinced me that it was a good idea.

Tucson was radically different from my native surroundings. Hotter, certainly, but maybe the most important difference was that the limits of town didn't seem to go on forever, with one suburb changing into the next without ever actually ending and transitioning into open space or wilderness. All of a sudden, there was the outdoors. The Sonoran desert surrounded us, and there were mountains right at the edge of town. It looked intriguing, but what to do about it? Hiking sounded easy enough; a pair of boots, a cloud of dust and a hearty "Hi-ho Silver!" and away you go, right?

Then again, it also sounded kind of like walking around with no particular purpose, and in a place where the temperature regularly went well over one hundred degrees, mildly suicidal. Experiencing the outdoors as a participant rather than just as an onlooker; now that sounded interesting, but where to start? I knew nothing of hunting or fishing.

Fate can be funny. A seemingly random craving for a cookie from Mrs. Fields can bring you face to face with a girl with big brown eyes and a smile that damn near kills you dead on the spot. Just like that, the rest of your life is determined by a chocolate chip cookie. When it comes to fishing, who knows? Maybe I would have found my way to it on my own eventually, but I didn't have to. Fate handed me a fly rod.

Clayton Nelson, my oldest childhood friend, was one of the people I knew who had headed out to Arizona for school. He lived a block away when we were kids, and I think we started playing together just after the fetal stage. He had been in Tucson for a year and he had already done some exploring with his dorm-mate, Jeff Garza. Jeff was an Arizona native who had grown up with fishing and hunting. He had shown Clay around some, and had introduced him to fly fishing.

Now if you spend enough time fly fishing, at some point in your life you may ask yourself if the person who introduced you to the sport really gave you a gift that keeps on giving for a lifetime, or if they are more like the dealer who got you hooked on coke, leaving you unable to get your mind off of rising trout and clear mountain streams for the rest of your life. In my case, the one who introduced me to fly fishing was Clay; but the source of the disease, the carrier, the alpha infection site for our little group, was Jeff Garza.

Learning to be an outdoorsman of any kind can be confusing for the newcomer. There are rules and traditions that need to be upheld. Take the practice of telling fish stories, for example. It's an art that takes time to perfect. The amateur will exaggerate at all the wrong points, leaving his audience with no choice but to disbelieve. Fish size is one of those areas that, while well understood by veteran outdoorsmen, can get the initiate in trouble quickly. Exaggerating the size of a single fish is common practice, and generally acceptable even if you push it to the limits of believability. Avoid your magical unicorns, and remember that two hundred pound tarpon don't swim in trout streams, and you should be okay. However, beware of telling your fishing buddies of a spot where all the fish are as long as your leg. You may have to back that up with evidence; which means taking your friends along so they can get some as well. When you are discovered, your credibility will be damaged for some time.

It's actually the details surrounding a trip where one can take the greatest liberties. Such things can be difficult, if not impossible to either prove or disprove. Add some adversity, maybe some danger, and you've got yourself a story. Maybe you happened to see a snake (of any kind); that could be reported as a near death experience with a den of rattlers. The truly talented storyteller could go almost so far as to expand the tale into an epic battle with the Midguard Serpent that would leave Thor himself feeling like less of a man.

Or, let's say that you have a couple of fishing buddies who went on a big fishing trip the previous summer (without you, of course). You can count on the fact that it will have been, without a doubt, The Greatest Adventure in The History of Mankind; eclipsing Columbus' journey to the New World, the Lewis and Clark expedition, and the Apollo lunar landing (combined), and thus worthy of dominating the discussion every time you get together. This was what it was like hanging out with Clay and Jeff throughout late 1992 and early 1993.

'92 was about when I first started going along on local trips to fish for bass or trout with spinning gear. Their "big fly fishing trip" had been outside my purview. It was a two-week trip through the Rocky Mountains (more or less), fishing and camping at one river for a couple of days before moving on to the next location. They had a favorite spot in southwestern Colorado on a relatively unknown stream that they talked about constantly in the closely guarded, hushed tones common to fishermen and inside traders, but the trip also included some famous trout rivers.

The plan for the coming summer was once again to fish through four states in just under two weeks. Among the better known destinations on the agenda were names like the Frying Pan in Colorado, the Green in Utah, and one in northern New Mexico that we had heard was pretty fair called the San Juan. None of those names meant anything to me back then, but Clay and Jeff planned to go one way or another, and they extended the invitation to come along.

The idea sounded strange at first. Life was pretty busy with school and work. I was having a good time slipping away to fish for a day here and there, but two weeks? That almost sounded like adding another commitment. It would be two unpaid weeks as well, and I wasn't exactly rolling in cash. Still, from the way they talked about this grand event over beer and pizza, I almost couldn't help myself.

If I was going to go, I would need to get a fly rod and to at least be sure I knew which end to hold. Getting a beginner's outfit for fly fishing isn't terribly expensive, but we were, after all, starving college students. Any outlay of cash beyond living expenses was always a big deal (yes, we considered beer and pizza a "living expense"); so, I did what any red-blooded American college student would do; I procrastinated until the last minute, and then made the (fateful) decision to go along.

Believe it or not, there was a fly shop in Tucson where I was able to get myself set up for the sum of about $150, which was pretty painful at the time. My first casting lesson came from Clay. He hadn't been at this for very long himself, but he was able to teach me the basic mechanics of casting. This didn't look anything like a high priced lesson on a casting pond behind a fly shop, mind you. Like most of our early efforts at fishing (or any other outdoor activity, for that matter), we improvised. It was around midnight on a weekday when we took my new rod and a six-pack out behind Clay's apartment complex to fly fish for bats.

Okay, there weren't any bats. Well, actually, there probably were some bats around, but we weren't trying to catch them. Anyway, it didn't take too long to get a feel for the basics, and a subsequent trip to fish the Salt River outside of Phoenix would give me the chance to practice on the water; but that was about all the time I had to prepare for my first foray into fly fishing.

The day of our trip arrived and I figured I was as ready as I could be. It was August of 1993, a few weeks before the start of the fall semester. I had my rod and reel, waders, and some clothes that seemed appropriate for the woods. At that point, I thought that flannel shirts were the ideal attire for fly fishing. That's what all the guys in the magazines were wearing at the time, anyway. I also thought that all trout streams must flow through high mountain settings, complete with pine trees and relatively cool temperatures. It actually took me many years to get over that notion, and to slowly break the habit of wearing flannel any time I was out fly fishing. I should have been over it after the first two days of our trip.

My ensemble was completed with a cheap pair of aviator-style polarized glasses, and the only kind of hat I had ever owned, an old red baseball cap. Clay and Jeff both brought along wide brimmed hats of some kind, and of course I had to give Clay some ribbing over it. He was a kid from Costa Mesa like me, and the only time you would have seen any kid we knew back in the day wearing a wide brimmed hat would be if they were dressed up as a cowboy for Halloween. I felt it was my duty to give him a hard time over this, California Dude to California Dude. It is interesting, though, to note how effective second degree burns on the tops of your ears can be at changing your opinion of wide brimmed hats. Approximately four days into the trip I decided they actually looked cool.

# New Mexico

## Trouble With Tailwaters

The San Juan River. The name of our first destination was virtually synonymous with great tailwater fishing back in 1993. The hype surrounding the place was monumental. Clay had clipped out a story from a sporting magazine about fishermen catching so many big fish that they were pulling their flies away from any trout that appeared to be under nineteen inches. Expectations were high. I hadn't caught too many big trout at that point. In fact, I think my total tally of trout that were larger than a typical pan-sized stocker was one. Like all of the fish I had caught up to that point, it had been taken on spinning gear and a lure.

The San Juan originates in the San Juan Mountains in Colorado, where (I'm told) you can find some reasonable freestone stream fly fishing. The tailwater section flows out of Navajo Reservoir just across the border in New Mexico. There's no missing the fact that you are in the desert at this point, and perhaps it wasn't exactly what I was expecting a great trout stream might look like. The section below Navajo Dam has an unmistakably southwestern feel, decorated primarily by scrub brush and just a few trees, and the braided runs of the river winding slowly between the high, rocky ledges of the canyon.

Our habit in those days was to drive all night at the beginning of a fishing trip. It makes perfect sense if you value extra fishing time over sleep. Well, it made sense at the time, anyway. So, after eleven hours on the road from Tucson to Navajo Dam, we managed to roll into Cottonwood Campground in the early morning hours, somewhere around 4:00 AM. After setting up camp, it was a short wait to get into one of the fly shops that are situated right next to the river. With newly purchased licenses in hand, we were ready to fish.

Summer fishing on the San Juan usually means hot, sunny days; and frequently a quick, violent afternoon thunderstorm. The water is always cold, which is probably the only thing that saved me from heat stroke considering my wardrobe selection. Within a couple of hours you could typically count on losing all feeling in your feet from the chilly water temperature.

The San Juan in those days was capable of drawing serious fly fishermen from all over the country, if not the world. I quickly realized that of all of my fly fishing fashion faux-pas, showing up at such a place wearing rubber waders may have been the worst. Suffice it to say that we were the lowest budget fishermen on the San Juan. Of course, at the time, the state-of-the-art was not yet the lightweight, breathable Gore-Tex we have today; it was neoprene, which, at least when used in hot weather to (presumably) keep one dry while wading, turned out to be a sadistic practical joke. But you looked cool if you had them...

We couldn't afford to hire a guide, which would have made quite a difference, I'm sure. We had to figure things out on our own. I could cast at this point, and I had some notion of how to achieve a (more or less) drag-free drift. I had really only practiced fishing with dry flies, which can work on the San Juan, but everyone was telling us that we would do better by going wet. On the recommendation of one of my companions, I started with a black wolly bugger, a pattern reputed to be at least somewhat effective on virtually anything with fins. Apparently no one told the trout at the San Juan. A few of them fled in terror at the sight of it, but as far as I could tell, most of them were laughing.

Clearly I was missing something. I was able to see plenty of trout, and they were nice big ones, too. They bore little resemblance to the comparatively dull-looking little stockers I had caught up until then. I could see twenty inch rainbows cruising in shallow water. Their backs were bright green and heavily spotted. They weren't feeding on top, aside from a very rare rise here and there. I guess it was enough to get me to switch back to fishing dry flies, but I wasn't able to fool any of them, or at least not in the light of day.

The only hook-up I got came around dusk, when the light was low enough to give me the advantage. The canyon walls and surrounding brush were already in darkness. There was enough light left to spot the rings of rising trout, and I could just pick out the silhouette of my oversized dry fly against the last of the red, yellow, and orange streaks of a desert sunset reflecting off of the water. What a picture perfect setting it would make for catching my first fish of the trip.

The pool was broad and slow-moving, and the fish didn't seem to be staying in a feeding lane, making them harder to target. I was using a size 14 Royal Wulff, a pattern that is unlikely to appear on anyone's list of recommended flies for fishing the San Juan.

I did my best to target the cruising trout, my eyes straining against the failing light to remain focused on the fly, which seemed determined to drift deftly in between the feeding fish while carefully avoiding being eaten. Then it happened. The head of a large rainbow come out of the water and calmly took my fly. I set the hook and felt the weight of the fish bending my rod. I had one on! I was not prepared for what happened next...

The thing went berserk; thrashing mightily before it turned and took off downstream. It was halfway to Lake Powell before I knew what was happening. The Pescado Diabolico was gone, along with my fly. The quick rush of adrenaline left me with my heart pounding and my hands shaking as I fumbled my way back to the truck in the dark. My one shot at a big San Juan Rainbow, and I lost it. Son of a....

Like many well-known streams, the San Juan has plenty of named pools; Texas Hole, Baetis Bend, the Hog Trough; they all sounded cool, except for the one I had been fishing. I got skunked at "The Kiddie Pool." Awesome.

Clay and Jeff had better luck than I did, but we didn't exactly slay 'em as a group. We hadn't planned on staying long at the San Juan, as my companions were anxious to get to their favorite little stream in Colorado. I really wanted another shot at those fish, but I had no idea of how to solve the riddle. As strange as it may sound, I didn't know how to fish a nymph. Either way, we were moving on, leaving me with only one option; like a cartoon super-villain denied success by a muscle-bound do-gooder in a leotard, I vowed to return and have my vengeance.

# Colorado

## Zen and the Art of Not Drowning

We were heading toward Telluride and the San Miguel River, which really isn't so much of a secret spot. There may not have been anyone else in Tucson who had ever heard of it, but everyone in southwestern Colorado knew it to be a solid little trout stream, though certainly not one that draws fishermen from far and wide.

The San Miguel turned out to be a much friendlier place to a beginning fly fisherman. It's a small free-flowing stream, very different from the tailwater fishery we had just come from. The scenery was much more in line with what I had been expecting; in other words mountains and pine trees. In the section we were fishing at least, it was relatively fast flowing, meaning all I had to do was put my dry fly in (approximately) the right place, and the trout would have to make a quick decision whether to eat it or not. After the intense cross-examination of my flies by the fish at the San Juan, some of whom I could have sworn were using a magnifying glass (while smoking a calabash pipe and jotting down notes in a notebook) before ultimately deciding to reject them; this was a favorable turn of events.

The San Miguel was also one of the few places on our itinerary where we planned to keep fish to eat. Finally, my companions knew of a secret spot to camp (this one really was a secret, or at least semi-secret) in an undeveloped site right on the river. No campground, no other fishermen. Looking back I can't say for sure if it was a legal place to set up camp, but back then I was a total neophyte and apparently was blissfully ignorant of such concerns.

The fishing was easy enough and good enough that I started catching trout pretty much right away. We fished primarily with dry flies and found the inhabitants willing to come up if you put the fly in the right spot. The fish were all moderately sized, but no one was bothered by the lack of truly large fish. My companions were busy clobbering fish at this little spot, and I was mostly left to figure things out on my own. No one held my hand just because I was new to all of this. I got a few pointers and that was about it. I was told to cast my dry fly as close to the banks as possible, and that turned out to be enough advice to get me into a few fish. Over a couple of days we caught plenty of trout, and ate our fill of pan-fried fish fresh from the river.

Over the years I've noticed that a pretty sizable number of folks seem to believe that fly fishermen are more like practitioners of a sort of stream-born transcendental meditation than they are people who are actually trying to catch a fish. I don't know about all that. I'm always trying to catch fish, though I would agree that there is quite a bit more in the appeal of fly fishing than simple catching. I can tell you, though, that if you're looking to have a Zen-like experience on the water, you're going to need to master the cast first. The Buddha himself might have a hard time maintaining inner peace while untangling wind-knots all day.

In fact, as far as I can tell, it is the cast itself that causes most of the fuss about fly fishing as a form of spiritualism. Seekers of truth, grace, and beauty can find at least two out of three of those things in a well-executed fly cast; and this leads many to believe that what they are witnessing couldn't possibly be something as simple as the act of relocating an artificial fly into a place where a trout might readily consume it.

As much as I'd like to say that we fly fisherman really are a bunch of Jedi Knights and fly casting can only be properly done by using The Force, in reality it isn't much different from anything else. With practice, casting begins to feel automatic, and the rod begins to obey your commands without you having to think about it too much, leaving you the option of allowing your mind to wander freely if you so desire. The San Miguel may have been the first place where I ever experienced being "in the zone", so to speak, but I am fairly certain that my potential one-ness with the universe never crossed my mind. Truth be told, my meditation didn't transcend much of anything. Like most men in their youth, my mind would tend to wander to thoughts of girls; which, if left unchecked, could lead to the disruption of an otherwise perfectly pleasant day of fishing. Perhaps contemplating one's navel really is the way to go after all.

Regardless of whether you believe that you are experiencing a higher plane of existence or just daydreaming, stepping in a deep hole and beginning to drift downstream as your rubber chest-waders quickly fill with water will snap you out of it in a hurry. All in all, aside from the initial shock, it wasn't so bad. After a few moments of half-swimming-half-stumbling I managed to right myself, then sloshed my way back to shore, waders full of ice-cold river water, where I proceeded to strip them off, dump them out, and go back to fishing.

Perhaps I didn't keep up with my more experienced companions, but at least I had started catching fish. In spite of dunking myself (Clay assured me that this sort of thing was to be expected, and informed me that both of my companions had destroyed fairly nice little cameras with similar episodes) I felt a whole lot more confident when the time came to move on to our next stop, the Frying Pan River above the town of Basalt, Colorado.

## Into The Frying Pan

The Frying Pan is another well-known tailwater fishery. We had all read about the place and knew it had some big fish, and likely some crowds.

Despite its' notoriety, the Frying Pan in those days felt fairly remote. The camping was done in a large, developed site next to Ruedi Reservoir, so it wasn't exactly deep wilderness, but still, at the time there wasn't much out there besides Basalt, and that wasn't much bigger than one grocery store, a hardware store, two fly shops, a motel, a gas station, and a smattering of various little shops. The whole town was about the size of a single city block.

The area has seen quite a bit of development since then, and doesn't feel particularly remote anymore. Back in the day, when we wanted a bite to eat, we stopped off at a little place called The Charburger, which looked like a shipping container with a grill, a bar, and some stools; but let me tell you what, they made a mean double cheeseburger. On my most recent trip we sat on the riverside deck of a nice restaurant and ate French fries drizzled with black truffle oil. It's a very different experience, but I have to admit, I think truffle oil could probably make an old shoe taste good, so I guess everything is a trade-off.

The Frying Pan flows thirteen miles from the base of the dam down through a (somewhat) steep canyon to the town of Basalt. The distinctive red rock cliffs make this one of the most scenic rivers in Colorado. The upper section of the river, within view of the dam, fishes like a classic tailwater. The fish can get really big in this section, though nothing we caught on this trip was in the huge category. Things change as you move downstream; one might even say that the river fishes more like a freestone stream once the dam is out of sight, and so one can experience two different types of fishing in a relatively short stretch of water.

Despite the reputation of fly fishermen as overt seekers of solitude, many of the trout streams of the Rocky Mountains end up being good places to meet interesting people. The cast of characters on the water our first morning at the Frying Pan certainly didn't disappoint. We were fishing a couple hundred yards downstream from the dam. There were plenty of other anglers out on the river that day, including a couple of old-timers. They appeared to be in their eighties. They were somewhat stooped over and didn't move around very well, and would have seemed more at home using a walker, or maybe a boy scout to help them cross the street. That all disappeared when they started casting. Their movements were quick and deliberate. Little more than a flick of the wrist sent tight-looped casts shooting from their ancient-looking bamboo rods. And let me tell you what, they were slayin' 'em. It felt a little like watching Yoda with a fly rod instead of a light saber. They were also ribbing each other like a couple of teenagers, proving once again that fishing is a great way to keep from ever growing up.

I watched intently, trying to learn from observation, while at the same time trying in vain to hook a fish myself. Then one of them ended up playing a brown of about eight pounds over toward me, landing it just a few feet away.

A young man's journey to becoming an angler wouldn't be complete without some input from an elder statesman of the sport. I guess it would be nice if we could all have Roderick Haig-Brown as a personal mentor, but you take what you can get. There are a few things to keep in mind as a would-be apprentice should you encounter an Old Master on the river. First, assume you are going to hear about how much better the fishing was before you were born. Consider it the price of admission. It's generally true, though occasionally the Ancient One will be talking about a river that was a warm-water mud-hole before the construction of the dam, which went up long after the "glory days" he is describing. There is no reason to point this out should you find yourself in such a situation. Old fishermen can be quite cagey. While he may indeed be getting senile, he may also think it's funny to let you think that he is. Some of these folks have also been known to lie to younger anglers for sport. You might not know the difference.

Trading fish stories is generally not recommended. It's best to just listen. Most importantly, under no circumstances should you attempt to "one-up" the Great Old One's fishing story. As impressive as it may be that you caught a ten pound rainbow on a four-weight, you will inevitably be humbled by his story of the twelve pound brown he caught while fishing with Ernest Hemingway in the middle of a fire-fight on the Italian Front during World War I.

"Nice fish." I offered, admiring the perfect specimen of a brown trout that it was.

"Yeah, there are some good ones in here." He replied in a raspy, grandfatherly voice.

"I'd love to catch one like that." I said.

"Let me show you a couple of things." He said as we started back toward his original spot.

"Cool." I replied.

"Say," he began as we walked back toward the hole, "Did I ever tell you about the time I fished the Miramichi with Ted Williams? Boy, could that guy cast a fly rod…"

Strange as it may sound, the Ancient Mariner wasn't the most memorable character on the river that day. In all fairness to my temporary mentor, it's not really all that unusual to run across old fishermen on a trout stream. Wheelchair-bound fly fishermen are a bit less common, though not unheard of. Still, I was pretty sure we had spotted a wheelchair access point not far from where we were fishing, but this guy wasn't using it. He was *wading*. We had no idea how he got there, or how he was going to get back out, but there he was. We could only assume he had help, because it didn't seem possible that he could have navigated a streambed with that thing. Even with help it didn't seem possible. As we stared in confused amazement, I felt the need to confirm that everyone else was seeing the same thing.

"How much Bourbon did I drink last night?" I asked Clay as I continued staring in disbelief.

"Not that much." He replied. "Why do you ask?"

"Oh, no reason. So, you're seeing this too, right? There's a guy wading in a wheelchair over there…"

"Yep."

"We are not worthy…"

As memorable as the morning was, something else was going on that I would prefer to forget. In spite of everything, I got skunked. Clay and Jeff both caught fish, but I couldn't manage so much as a single take from the finicky fish in the upper river.

We spent most of our time on the Frying Pan fishing the lower river. I had a little bit of luck early on with some smaller fish in pocket water, as did my companions. We were prospecting, covering as much ground as we could before heading back to the truck to find another stretch of river and start the process over again. Somewhere in the mid to lower part of the river I got set up on a pool that looked particularly fishy. It was broad and deep in the middle, where the current was heavy. There was a large sunken boulder disrupting the flow right in the center of the pool. It was a shady spot with a rock cliff on the far side, heavy tree cover, and a seemingly endless patch of horrific thorn bushes lining the sides of the stream so that getting in or out was difficult for several hundred yards.

I liked the look of the hole and decided to fish it thoroughly while Clay and Jeff started working their way upstream. I had a hopper pattern tied on and decided to go with it. I wanted to see if there was a fish behind that rock. Everybody had told me that trout like to hold behind rocks, so there should be a big one behind the big rock, right? I just had to figure out how to roll cast and I could find out.

Maybe it wasn't terribly pretty, but after a few attempts I managed to get my fly out far enough to get a drift over the rock, only to find that I couldn't keep it afloat. The swirling currents around the rock were conspiring against me, and my fly was pulled under quickly. So much for my plan.

I had only a moment to contemplate how to adjust my drift before I noticed that my line was swimming away on its own, or so it seemed. I lifted the rod and was tight to a fish that had a head of steam behind it. It was pulling quite a bit harder than the small ones I had picked up so far; this had to be a better fish.

I'd been obsessing over that one big fish I'd lost at the San Juan since it happened; waiting for my shot at redemption. I knew what was plaguing me. Those first few seconds after a big fish takes can make or break the entire affair. What do you do with all the slack line? Surely this is the most confusing part of fly fishing for the newcomer. It certainly was for me. It just doesn't seem natural. With any other type of fishing, you start reeling when you hook a fish. With a fly rod, you set the hook, and you're holding the line, and there might be piles of it all around you, just waiting to get caught on whatever might be about. What do you do? If the trout runs and you're fishing a light tippet, you have to give him line in a way that mimics a well-set drag. Well, that's no problem at all for a beginner, right? Then there's the moment when you run out of slack line and it hits the reel. Again, if you're using light tippet, this is often the point when it breaks. I knew that was how I had lost that fish at the San Juan. These days, high-end reels have a "zero inertia" feature (not to mention drags so smooth you could probably land a blue whale on 6X tippet if you only had the patience for it), but I had an old-school click and pawl type reel, which meant that the drag was (pretty much) the palm of your hand.

The trout ripped downstream, using the heavy current to his advantage. There was no time to think about what to do. He had taken all the slack line and was on the reel, which was now screaming as the fish sped away, before I knew what had happened.

I'd had some practice since the San Juan, and I felt much more confident, even though nothing I'd landed so far was of any substantial size. I hadn't actually tried palming the reel yet, though I'd seen it done. I had to do something quick, before the fish went around the next bend and swam away with my fly line in tow. I gently pressed my palm against the spinning reel…

It worked! I was able to slow him down, and eventually turn him around. It seemed to me like the fight lasted quite some time, but in reality it was probably over in just a minute or two. After the first long run, I was able to slowly work him back into the soft water along the edge of the pool and land him.

Maybe fly fishing is a more appropriate pursuit for quiet, contemplative types than adrenaline junkies, but it has its' moments. My heart was pounding. My hands were shaking. As much as I wanted to let out a shout, I resisted; though at that moment I felt like a kid who'd just hit his first Little League home run.

Looking back now, an eighteen inch rainbow doesn't seem particularly large, but it might as well have been Moby Dick at the time. And the colors; all of a sudden the name rainbow trout made perfect sense.

I'm pretty sure Clay was the first one out of the dugout to offer me a high-five when I actually did hit my first Little League home run; but this time no one had been there to witness my moment of triumph, much less snap a picture for posterity. All there was to do was to absorb the moment as well as I could. A quarter century later the images in my mind are a little cloudy; maybe I can't picture the fish as it truly was; and the spot… I might not be able to find it on the river anymore. But I can still feel it.

I was too excited to continue fishing. I had to find the guys and tell them about the fish. The thorn bushes prevented me from following on land, so I stumbled upstream against the current as quickly as I could, and found them fishing together, pounding the banks with dry flies, and covering ground quickly.

"Hey guys, I finally got a big one!" I called out.

"Sweet." Clay replied. "How big was it?"

"About eighteen."

"Nice fish." Jeff added. "On a dry fly?"

"Sure, if you count a sunken grasshopper as a dry."

"We should celebrate." Clay replied.

Celebrating didn't mean a party; nor did it mean a Gatorade bath from a dugout full of team-mates. It certainly didn't mean a champagne toast. We went with what we had, which was a solid supply of Jim Beam. It also seemed to my companions that this was as good a time as any to break out their campground dinner specialty.

Our campground fare was generally pretty simple in those days. We ate a lot of canned items, including beef stew, chili (sometimes cold right out of the can for lunch, which isn't so bad once you get past the coagulated grease), potatoes, vegetables, you name it. About the only thing that didn't come out of a can was fresh caught trout. The "dinner special" that Clay and Jeff had planned for that night was a particularly disturbing tradition that they had established the year before. They called it chili surprise. It consisted of canned chili, beef stew, canned corn, canned tamales, and canned potatoes all combined into one pot. And the secret ingredient: a pinch of Copenhagen. Not enough to cause any real adverse effects, it was just in there to mess with your head.

"Uh-huh." I commented when I found out what they had planned. "Let's flambé the whole thing with Bourbon."

"Dude!?!" Clay replied (translation: What the (#%$*!!?))

"Dude." I answered back (translation: What's the problem, man?)

"Dude!" Clay reiterated (translation: Don't mess with the chili surprise. It's a tradition. And besides, this stuff is nearly indigestible. You're going to kill us.)

"Dude." I replied (translation: I've got this. It's going to make it better.)

"Can you actually do that?" Jeff interjected.

"Dude, you can flambé with pretty much anything that has enough alcohol in it. I do it at work all the time... Dude."

"Dude..." Clay offered in resignation (translation: Whatever, man.)

Chili surprise was, of course, more of a test of manhood than it was an actual means of sustenance. This concoction was best consumed in the dark, so one wasn't looking at the Frankenstein's monster of a dish that it was. Strangely, my version tasted mostly like Bourbon. Oh, well. Even pot luck from a can tastes pretty good around a camp fire.

## The Lake: There Can Be Only One

We had one more stop in Colorado: Trapper's Lake. It had been on the itinerary from the previous year and the guys said that the dry-fly fishing had been outstanding. It also had some seriously spectacular scenery. Ten thousand feet in elevation, with mountains and trees as far as the eye could see. At night the Milky Way was clearly visible, and there were so many stars that the sky almost looked white with little patches of black sprinkled in rather than the other way around. (At least at the time) I'd never seen anything quite like it.

Trapper's Lake also boasts the largest population of native Colorado River cutthroat trout in the world. We were there to catch fish on dries, so we focused on the early morning and late afternoon hours. Unfortunately for us, the lake was like glass in the morning, and the trout were not very cooperative. The afternoon was a different story. There was just enough of a breeze to put a little ripple on the surface of the lake. By the time the afternoon shadows were beginning to appear, we started catching trout on top. With perfect conditions like these, all we really had to do was cast our flies out and wait.

There was something different about our fishing experience at Trapper's Lake versus the rest of the trip. We were fishing together, and I was catching fish at the same rate as my companions. So, the fishing wasn't particularly challenging, that wasn't enough to ruin the moment for me, the greenhorn of the group. Maybe it caught Jeff a bit by surprise to see his padawan learner keeping up with him, but it was impossible not to have a good time, and we all caught medium-sized cutthroats until the sun went down. If it occurred to me to count how many fish I caught, I must have lost track at some point. Clay didn't, though, and he refused to be dragged off the water before landing his twentieth.

Experience will eventually teach you that the woods are full of natural booby-traps, but I was still, after all, pretty new to all of this; and as much as the fishing may have been going well, I didn't make it through this stop totally unscathed. As I was walking along the shore of the lake looking for a good place to fish I came to a small feeder stream. It would be easy enough to simply jump over, and so I figured I would do just that. I took one step, planted my foot for launch, and instantly sank in the mud clear up to the top of my thigh.

To say the least, I was caught off guard, and a bit freaked out. The other leg wasn't in nearly as deep, but I couldn't find anything to plant it against to push myself out, and there was nothing I could reach to pull free with either. I was stuck.

I briefly considered calling for help; but since I wasn't sinking (at least for the moment), trying to come up with a creative way to free myself seemed like the better plan. There may not have been any You Tube at the time, but we did have cameras, and having the moment preserved for posterity was something I hoped to avoid. As it turned out, this was the one conceivable situation in which rubber waders proved to be an advantage. They are, after all, far from form-fitting. In fact, I was able to wriggle out of them and free myself. The waders weren't even all that hard to pull free once my weight was no longer in them, and I was left with very muddy waders, but none the worse for wear.

# Utah

### A Great Place to Grab A Beer...

By the time we decided to move on to our next stop, I had come to the conclusion that Colorado had to be the epicenter of mountains, streams, and trout; which made it difficult to leave. But, we were on our way to another famous trout stream, the Green River below Flaming Gorge Reservoir, just across the border in Utah. This meant another change of scenery, back to high desert and colorful rock formations.

The first thing I noticed about Utah (or rather the tiny little towns along the highway as one nears the border of Utah) is that the liquor stores in said tiny towns can seem, shall we say, a bit disproportionately large. This factoid doesn't necessarily make it into travel guides, but is darn convenient when you're running low on beer and Bourbon.

Another thing I noticed, which has held true throughout the years, is that trout streams rarely flow through ugly landscapes. Even so, there are some that stand out, and the Green is one of those. With the possible exception of the Lee's Ferry stretch of the Colorado, I know of no other trout stream with a canyon quite so spectacular.

Flaming Gorge Dam rises five hundred feet above the river, which carves its' way through the deep red rock canyon below, where Pinyon Pines and Junipers sprout from the craggy face of the cliffs. The first few miles below the dam are loaded with trout, including some real hogs.

There is plenty of bank access along the seven and a half miles from Flaming Gorge Dam down to Little Hole, and we hiked most of it. I guess that strikes me as a bit ironic, given my lack of enthusiasm for taking up hiking as a hobby. And let's just say that if someone had told me that the way to really enjoy hiking is to be sure to do it in the desert in the middle of August; but also to first properly outfit yourself by donning sweat pants and a flannel shirt, and then slipping into a chest-high rubber suit, I'm pretty sure that would have failed to inspire greater interest in the whole affair on my part.

All I can say is that it's funny what you will put up with when said hike gives one access to great trout water. Of course it helps to be in your early twenties, when your ability to withstand physical hardship leads you to believe that you are invincible; or at the very least that you can replace the ten pounds of water weight lost in a day with beer and beef stew from a can by the end of the evening.

I can't remember if it occurred to us to wade wet, and if it did, why we decided against it. Aside from the typically chilly water temperatures common to tailwaters, I can't think of a good reason. You know, I don't remember if wet wading was "a thing" at the time. If so, we probably didn't know it, though there must have been some people who did it. It's not like you *had* to wait for someone to come up with wet wading socks and full-length khaki swim trunks before you were allowed to enter a trout stream without waders.

Oh well. I suppose we could have packed them in, but rubber chest waders are *bulky*... they don't pack-in so well. Besides that, we were prospecting, as usual. We would fish a good looking spot, then hike until we found another, so it seemed that keeping them on made more sense.

So it is with fly fishermen and their waders. After the fly rod itself, they're just about your most indispensable piece of gear. But, as I was quickly learning, the relationship is... complicated. Anyone who's ever peeled off their neoprene waders at the end of a day to find that they had (technically) "worked" to keep river water out, but had trapped enough sweat to leave them drenched anyway; or had to slip on Gore-tex waders first thing on a chilly morning while they are still *frozen solid* will understand. Of course, both neoprene and Gore-tex are luxurious compared to rubber.

So, it should come as no surprise when some member of the group comes up with a fitting nickname as you're sitting in camp sipping coffee and gearing up for the day; excited for the fishing, yet simultaneously staring apprehensively at the piles of sweat-soaked rubber, fully aware of the price that has to be paid.

"Well gentlemen, it's time to don the iron maidens."

What can I say? Sometimes you just nail it.

It was back to struggling to catch fish for me as the trout at the Green River were quite a bit more selective than the cutthroats at Trapper's Lake. Clay and Jeff did better, including a really nice brown that Jeff caught that was probably the biggest fish of the trip. Our official fish-size committee decided it was two feet long, though no one had a tape measure and our ability to guess fish sizes really wasn't particularly well calibrated. It was a beauty, one way or another.

I just wanted to get *one*. That way I wouldn't have to add another name to The List. At one point I spotted what appeared to be a pretty nice trout rising right off of the far side of a huge boulder. I could see it coming up, but I would need to somehow curve a cast around the rock to get the fly in front of him. If I could wade out just a bit farther maybe I could get the angle, but it looked pretty deep out there.

One more step proved to be one too many, and this time I was treading water in a bigger river with powerful, swirling currents that had a reputation for drowning the occasional angler who didn't take it seriously. There was no way to regain my footing. I had to swim for it, and do it quickly as my waders once again filled with water.

Again, I didn't die. I didn't even lose my fly rod. Being soaking wet wasn't even too much of a hardship considering the August heat at the Green. I learned my lesson about wading after that.

All of these events happened over twenty years ago, making it difficult to remember much about the specifics of conversations that were had around the campfire, with a few notable exceptions. While sitting around the fire on our last night at the Green, Jeff was the first one to bring up the one thing we all were thinking, but didn't necessarily want to say.

"Well boys, our trip is winding down."

Something about hearing it said out loud made it feel all the more unavoidable. I felt like a kid whose parents had just said it was time to leave Disneyland, and I guess it must have caught me off-guard. After all, I'd been skunked as often as not, and always at the places with the biggest fish. I'd fallen in three different rivers. I'd gotten myself stuck in quick-mud. I had second-degree blistering sun burns on the tops of my ears. As if that weren't enough, the three of us had been sharing Jeff's little 7' x 7' Coleman tent (that was supposedly considered a "three man" tent, though I'd like to see how the math works out on that) for the better part of two weeks, without access to showers for any of it. It was starting to get a bit ripe in there.

Not that I was complaining. Besides, based on the only book I'd ever read about camping (Patrick McManus' *A Fine and Pleasant Misery*) it seemed like all of this meant that we were doing it right (no offense intended to the iconic Mr. McManus, but the first thing on my list of gear to pick up for next year was still going to be a (much) bigger tent). Anyway, the point is that I was having the time of my life. I wasn't ready for it to end.

I had another list that I was formulating as well, my Secret Evil Plan for Vengeance Against Trout, which now had three names on it: San Juan, Frying Pan, and Green. Looking back, I suppose you would have to say that the Frying Pan had been pretty good to me, but watching all those big fish that first morning in the upper river and being unable to hook even one had stuck in my craw, so, well, it had to be on there too.

## Last Stop, Provo

The plan had been to get a motel room at our last stop, the Provo River. Provo, Utah was only a little bit out of the way, and would put us back on the main highway for our trip south. The camping part of our trip was done, but take-out pizza never tasted so good, and the only bar in town took the place of a campfire. Yes, there was a bar in Provo, complete with bartenders who were licensed and registered with the state. There's just something compelling about finding a place to get a drink in Utah, or at least it seems that way when you're in your early twenties.

You would think we would have gotten up and hit it hard for our last day of fly fishing, but all I can say is that we must have been tired. By the time we dragged ourselves out of bed, consumed the last of the cold pizza, and schlepped ourselves down to the river, there wasn't even all that much time to fish. The Provo River deserved better. It was a little gem, and we all caught some nice trout. The browns were particularly pretty.

The end of the day brought with it a finality that couldn't be avoided. The journey home was to begin the next morning. It was there again; that feeling, like I was six years old, playing and having the time of my life, and then I heard my mom's voice saying it was time to go. I guess it still surprised me. Of course the adult (fisherman) equivalent of "Just five more minutes, Mom" is "One more cast…"; but we all wrap it up at some point, even if it's just because it's too dark to continue. As I put away my fly rod for the journey, all I could think about was how my Great Adventure was at an end, and I didn't want it to be.

## Arizona

### One long-ass drive please, and a medium order of trout on the side…

The drive from Provo to Tucson is about twelve and a half hours without stops, and we had one important stop to make. I guess it wasn't quite accurate to say that the Provo River was our final destination. If we got going early enough we could make it to Lee's Ferry in time to fish for a while before the final leg of the drive.

Lee's Ferry is the name of a section of the Colorado River just below Lake Powell in northern Arizona. A sunken river ferry once belonging to a Mormon settler by the name of John D. Lee sits at the bottom of the river where you can see it clearly from shore, hence the name. This is the beginning of the Grand Canyon, so needless to say it is picturesque. It seemed a fitting location for our last few hours of fishing.

We didn't wader up, and we didn't break out the fly rods; we just walked the bank blasting out Kastmasters and other assorted types of hardware with spinning rods. The idea was to pick up a few nice fish quickly to help break up the drive, and it worked like a charm. We all caught fat, healthy rainbows for a couple of hours before we had to start the final leg of the trip, approximately seven hours back to Tucson.

Yes, Fate is a funny thing. When I was a kid, my mother signed me up for lessons in just about everything she could find. Team sports may have occupied most of my time, but I also took classes in gymnastics, swimming (everyone in SoCal learned to swim), bowling, drawing, acting, kung-fu, guitar, archery, sailing, tennis, and surfing. None of it really stuck, though I still like to shoot a bow from time to time. Then I went and moved off to the desert and picked up fly fishing, and I've never put it down.

Over the next year I would spend (somewhat unreasonable) amounts of time plotting, scheming, and accumulating everything I would need to go on my Vengeance Tour to all of the same rivers. I found it hard to keep my mind off of wilderness and trout, and I went fishing whenever I got the chance. I suppose not much has changed over the twenty-something years since, though I'd like to think I've become a better fisherman. I don't fall in as much, anyway.

We all went on the "big fishing trip" one more time the next summer before going our separate ways after graduation. I dragged my brother Chris along on that one, and yes, fly fishing has ruined his life too. Oh wait, I mean, he has found a lifelong passion for beautiful fish, wilderness, and adventure, just like the rest of us.

## Trout Wars: Return of the Angler

For some people, learning to fly fish means taking some pricey casting lessons on a perfectly manicured lawn next to a posh fishing lodge, followed by a ride in a drift boat with a guide who can do just about everything for you in exchange for a measly few hundred dollars. For others, it was Dear Old Dad who taught them the ways of the fly rod, no doubt creating memories to be treasured for a lifetime.

For a few of us, it was a self-taught, trial-and-error based series of underfunded misadventures beset by skunks, rattlesnakes, quick-mud, and the spines of several species of cactus; often involving fishless days, some fishless nights, brushes with dehydration and drowning, countless sleep-deprived hours of driving, sleeping in the cabs of (small) trucks, and frustrated vows to give up fishing. Of course, top of the line gear would have no place in such a scenario, but rubber chest waders are right at home. Perhaps the one bright side of doing it the hard way like that is that you can look back at the experience and tell yourself that you paid your dues.

In spite of all of that, and even in the midst of your suffering for fish, you might be lucky enough to have an adventure that resets your perspective; on fishing and perhaps on your entire life. So it was with my first real fly fishing trip; a barnstorming two week adventure through the Rocky Mountains. The year was 1993, and starting from Tucson, our small, rag-tag band of broke college students made a big loop through New Mexico, Colorado, and Utah.

The trip was a mixed bag for me, at least in terms of fishing success. I was a complete novice, trying to learn as I went. I did reasonably well in the more freestone(ish) places, but the highly technical tailwater fishing gave me fits. My more experienced companions did better, and there were people around us catching some real beasts. I vowed to return the next year and even the score on all of those rivers.

One of those places was the Frying Pan River in Colorado. Among the most famous of tailwaters, it hosts a population of trout with Ph.Ds. in fake food identification. I found the lower stretches manageable, but in the upper section, within view of the dam, where many of the largest, most finicky trout dwell; that was a different story. I couldn't coax so much as a tail swat out of those fish. You'd have thought I was dragging a rusty muffler from a '59 Edsel across the water; except that the muffler might have worked better.

Well, I went on that redemption tour the next year, and it worked out even better than I had hoped, in every location except one; the Frying Pan. My plan was foiled by the high-season crowds. We moved on out of frustration before I could accomplish my mission.

Four more years passed before I developed a renewed appetite for that plate of cold revenge. I had moved to Colorado by then, and could make the trip whenever I chose. We decided late spring would be the perfect time, when schizophrenic weather helps keep sane people off the water.

It felt like summer that morning as we drove the last few yards of the red dirt road to the parking area not far below Ruedi Dam. Technically it was still spring, but the sky was clear blue, and even the tallest of the surrounding forested peaks were free of snow. As predicted, there were just a few other anglers around. We walked in near the bottom of the pool, a few hundred yards below the dam. It didn't take long to spot a trout rising regularly against the far bank. I turned to my (now ex) wife, who was my fishing companion pretty regularly in those days;

"You see that fish rising over there?" I asked Laura.

"Yeah, I see it." She replied.

"What do you want to bet I can catch it with one cast?" I offered with Ruthian bravado.

"Okay, show me." She said.

I studied the rising trout as I peeled line off of my reel. When I felt like I had the timing down I started casting. He was right up against the brush-lined bank, the cast would need to be well timed and accurate. I watched him come up one last time, then flipped my dry fly a few feet ahead of him. It landed perfectly and drifted down toward the fish, which rose right on time, and took the fly as unsuspectingly as a baby taking a bottle from Mommy. Mommy set the hook.

I looked over at Laura with a self-satisfied expression. I was feeling pretty cocky at that moment. Five years earlier this had all seemed like some sort of sorcery. I had stood there watching my flies drift along without arousing the slightest interest from the trout, while an old man just upstream of me caught fish one after another like it was child's play.

The old man was a memorable character. He and his equally proficient (and equally elderly) fishing buddy put on a clinic on the river that day in 1993. To look at them you would worry about one of them falling and being unable to get up, yet once in the water they fished rings around everyone else out there. He was a very nice guy, and even offered me some advice; but whatever he was doing, I couldn't replicate it. It seemed clear enough to a kid from the Star Wars generation that he was using The Force, and if he had held out his hand and levitated fish out of the water I would have been only mildly surprised.

With the fish still on the line I turned to Laura, unable to resist offering up my best Darth Vader impression;

"The circle is now complete. When I left here I was but the learner, now I am the master."

I got no more than an eye-roll for what seemed to me to have been a particularly clever line. What can I say? Sometimes your best material goes unappreciated.

Speaking of the old man, he had appeared to be in his eighties back in '93, so there was no knowing if he was still alive. Just then I half expected to see his ghost in the river, decked out in Jedi robes and glowing ever so slightly.

The rest of the morning was filled with catching similar fish, mostly browns in the seventeen to eighteen inch range, but the really big boys were conspicuously absent. It was late in the day when I finally spotted one, sipping tiny dry flies in shallow water up against the far bank.

Just when you think you have trout behavior figured out, like when you brag that you can catch a trout with one cast and actually pull it off, they'll remind you of exactly what sort of enigmatic creatures they can be. I put (what appeared to be) a perfect imitation of the naturals in front of that fish a gazillion times (give or take). I had the timing down. My tippet was the diameter of spider silk. The trout wasn't fooled.

Surface feeding trout ought to be a relatively straight-forward affair, particularly if you've ever dealt with steelhead. The steelhead isn't even hungry, yet you have to convince them to eat something that (many times) doesn't look like anything, much less food. Some say they strike out of anger or territorial instinct. Okay, but if someone waved something that looked somewhat like the flag of Bolivia (and not in the least like, say, a burger and fries) in your face until you became irritated, would you try to eat it?

I'm not sure how long I stuck with it. Was it ten minutes or two hours? Time is relative when one is sight casting to a feeding trout. It's kind of like travelling at the speed of light in Special Relativity, only less… impossible. I persisted, watching the little mayfly imitation drift down the seam again and again, right over the fish each time. It ignored them all, occasionally taking flies that were close enough that they appeared to be attempting to mate with my imitation. Again, and again, and again.

The take, when it finally came, was so casual that you would have to believe that the fish didn't suspect a thing.

After all that, the fight was almost anticlimactic. Either way, the fish was a real beauty; twenty-two inches and heavy, adorned with spots from top to bottom, and in full spawning array; with an olive-green back, a bright red stripe, and gill plates to match.

I admired the fish for a moment, thinking about how much things had changed. The strange sorcery of catching trout on flies made sense to me now. Well, for the most part anyway. I had accomplished the thing that I came for, the redemption that had seemed so important but had eluded me four years earlier. Perhaps it was just a small personal victory, but if you can't enjoy those, life can get pretty mundane. Even Luke Skywalker doesn't blow up the Death Star every day. Speaking of which, I was half expecting to hear the ghostly voice of the old fisherman whispering: "The Force will be with you always" in my ear as I released the fish back into the chilly waters of the Frying Pan.

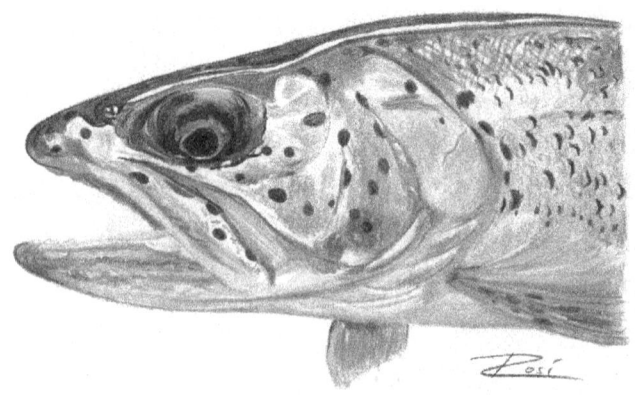

## Don't Be So Negative

Very few things will teach you to anticipate problems like a series of ill-fated fishing trips. Maybe that explains why those of us who learned to fly fish through trial and error seem to develop quasi-psychic powers over time. No, I can't predict the future per se, so don't ask me for sports picks. I can only see impending mishaps, from the minor to the disastrous, coming when no one else can.

This might sound pretty cool, but let me assure you, it's tough being "that guy". You know, the guy who says: "Hang on a second" when everyone else is ready to charge the hill. It doesn't really matter if you're just warning your friends about the tribulations of wilderness fishing trips, or if you're saying that writing billions of dollars' worth of sub-prime loans to people who can't really afford to pay them back might not be such a good idea. You end up hearing: "Oh, don't be so negative" either way. Eventually you learn to keep quiet most of the time, and find a secluded corner to bang your head against a wall when the entire economy collapses and government experts claim that no one could have predicted it.

Of course, even the most disastrous fishing trip is unlikely to tank the nation's economy; so, if your friends insist on embarking on one that's sure to include learning some lessons the hard way, you can still go along and rest (reasonably) assured that you'll probably come away with nothing more serious than a story to tell…

In the summer of 1999, my (now ex) wife and I started spending time with another couple I knew from work, who happened to be outdoorsy in a generic, somewhat unfocused way. They particularly loved high mountain lakes. One of their favorite things was to spend the evening playing with their dogs around one of the many lakes in the mountains near Denver. As the sun sank, the water would come alive with rising trout, but they had never tried to catch one. I had a young black Labrador who liked to play in the water as well, but when we came along I also brought a fly rod. Just one bejeweled little brookie was all it took. The epiphany was virtually instantaneous.

Soon my new protégés wanted to fish constantly. My own plans to explore Colorado's alpine lakes had been on the back burner for years, and now I had the perfect excuse. On weekday evenings we fished dry flies for brookies and rainbows in Brainard or Red Rock Lake in the mountains above Boulder. On our days off, we searched the beaver ponds of Rocky Mountain National Park for the elusive greenback cutthroat.

As the summer went on, our desire for seclusion and remoteness drove us farther into the wilderness, where only those willing to leave the beaten path will ever cast a line, and those with an appetite for solitude and spectacular scenery can find fulfillment. Each trip had to one-up the last. To cap off the summer, we would need a place so remote that it bordered on the absurd. That was when we heard about Little Echo Lake.

According to the guy at the Bucking Brown Trout Fly Shop in Nederland, it was a small alpine lake near James Peak. To find it we would need a GPS, and to even get close, a four wheel drive vehicle. A hike in was required. What he told us about the fly fishing sounded a little hard to believe, but he was clear about bringing some black ant patterns if we were going to fish it in August.

It was too intriguing. We had to plan an outing as soon as possible to fish the place. We were able to find it without too much trouble, and the hike wasn't too bad either (at least with only fly rods and float tubes to carry), though it did include an extended uphill climb to get back to the truck.

A glacial aquamarine-colored pothole carved out of bare rock, Little Echo Lake butts up against the sheer side of the mountain right around timberline, where patches of snow persist even in August. It's no more than fifteen acres, but our informant claimed it was more than one hundred feet deep. It wasn't too hard to believe. You got the sense looking down from a float tube into it's semi-turbid depths that it was bottomless. I suppose that could be a bit disconcerting if you were to dwell on it; the notion that there might actually be room to hide Cthulhu down there.

We had our flying black ant patterns ready, and to our delight, the fly shop guy had been telling the truth. The moderately sized (mostly twelve to fourteen inch) fish that were happily feeding on the surface were lake trout. Yes, I mean mackinaw, Salvelinus namaycush, taking dry flies. Cool.

We spent the afternoon blissfully catching the peculiar little lakers. It was the pinnacle of a summer of alpine adventure that, at least for me, a moving water guy at heart, would never be replicated. But it wasn't enough. We had to go back, only this time everybody wanted to camp. I couldn't help myself…

"Hey guys," I offered as gently as I could, "This sounds great and all, but I don't have mountaineering gear. All of my camping gear is bulky. That hike is gonna be a lot harder. Not to mention the altitude. It could get dicey up there."

"Oh, don't be so negative!" was the (completely predictable) reply.

I was only trying to protect *them*. It wasn't so much that anyone was really out of shape, but perhaps not quite in prime physical condition either. With all the gear we would need to carry, one (or more) of them might collapse from a walk around the block, much less an uphill hike. They also seemed to be expecting idyllic camping conditions, complete with roasting marshmallows over a fire under starry skies. I was picturing how much wind it would take to make trees grow horizontally.

Then again, whether you're steelheading in sub-zero temperatures in eastern Washington, or hiking around an Arizona bass lake all day in 115 degree heat with a two-inch Saguaro spine lodged in your calf, suffering for fish is just part of the game. They had to learn it sometime. As for me, I had a Ph.D. in Suffering for Fish, acquired through many years of doing stupid things in order to catch fish. One more time wouldn't kill me.

Maybe they started to understand what I had been trying to say when they saw how much crap we would have to carry, but by then we were committed. I had a change of clothes and some food and water in my backpack, to which was lashed a fully inflated float tube, a (large) sleeping bag, waders, wading boots, a fly vest, a rod and reel, float tube flippers, and my old Coleman 10' x 10' dome tent (which weighed twenty pounds on its own).

I didn't press the point about what we were getting into, as it was certain to be met with another remark about having a bad attitude...

We couldn't keep the fire going. The wind was ripping through our campsite, causing all manner of mayhem. My old camp stove might have gotten the job done, but it was ten pounds of metal, and burgers can be cooked right over a fire... if you have a fire. Now we couldn't eat.

All there was to do was to hide in the tent; which, as we quickly discovered, would have worked as a headsail on a fifty-foot sloop. Most of the night was spent holding it off from smothering us, but every so often the wind would catch it just right, and it seemed very much like we might actually blow away, even with four adults, three large dogs, and all of our gear in there with us.

The next morning we dragged ourselves to the lake and spent the day tooling around in our float tubes until it was painfully obvious that the flying black ants were gone. That left the hike back up the mountain. Rest stops were every thirty seconds or so, and the gear load was redistributed so that I ended up dragging an extra float tube behind me. That ruined it, of course, but it was still better than having to drag out a body had anyone actually dropped dead.

I've never experienced the sensation that I could take off and fly as strongly as I did the moment I stripped all that crap off of my back.

Can't say I didn't warn them, but when you're "that guy", it sometimes feels like you could warn someone not to pick up a live cobra and still hear about how you have a bad attitude. It's my own fault. Try as I might, I just can't seem to grasp the notion that vetting ideas is really just negative thinking. Thank goodness for the outdoors, the tried-and-true proving ground for Murphy's Law, where folks who think that all they need is a positive attitude are often the first ones to be eaten by wolves.

Anyway, no one died, and the economy didn't collapse, so it's all good. Then again, now that I think about it, the economy did collapse starting early the next year. The so-called "Dot-com Bubble". No one could have predicted that one either. Right. We need more fly fishermen running this country.

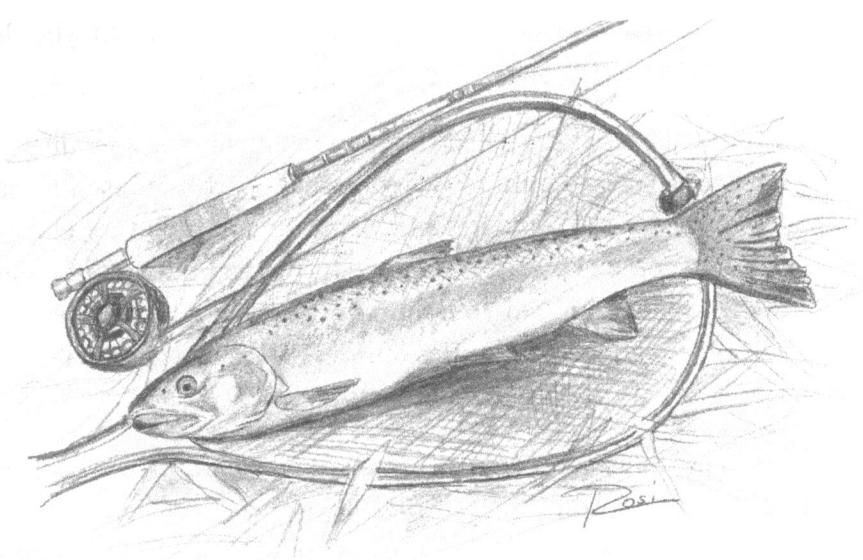

# Born Again

Fly fishing has a tendency to produce fanatics, purists, and even some insufferable snobs. Sure, not everyone who picks up a fly rod goes down those paths, but it does seem that the percentage of practitioners of the long rod who are casual about it is lower than with other forms of fishing. From the moment I first picked up a fly rod, I knew I was onto something that was more than a passing interest. Fly fishing captured my imagination. I read books about it, I hung out in fly shops talking about it, I was always planning my next trip, and if there was a free day that could have been spent fishing but wasn't, I would be grumpy about it.

Apart from some of the snobbery that I tried hard to avoid, practically everything about fly fishing appealed to me. But sometimes even the things you really love can start to lose their luster. So what happens when you wake up one day and you realize that you just aren't as motivated to get up and go fishing as you once were? Do you just chalk it up to being older and busier? There's nothing unique about that, after all the bell of responsibility eventually tolls for every fisherman, except maybe John Gierach.

Maybe what you really need is a new challenge; a new quarry to pursue, maybe some new terrain to re-ignite that spark you used to have. You could go looking for something like that; maybe plan an elaborate fishing vacation to some exotic destination. Or, life can put you in the path of something like that coming to you; migrating through the dark waters of the Pacific Ocean, up hundreds of miles of river, through a gauntlet of man-made dams, to arrive a short drive from your door.

My decade long campaign of assault on the trout of the Rocky Mountains drew to a close in the fall of 2005, when I relocated to Walla Walla, Washington. Come to think of it, the assault probably felt more like an occasional annoyance to the trout in my favorite streams for those last few years. The transformation (from a gung-ho twenty-something fly fisherman not long out of college who chose Colorado as a home base primarily for the fly fishing, to a responsible thirty-something business person who did little else besides work) was nearly complete. My six day work week left little time for fishing, and when I did get a free day I was often too tired to do anything about it. Still, it seemed like there was more to my situation than simple time and energy issues. I was lacking motivation. It seemed that the challenge and the mystery of catching trout on flies wasn't quite what it was in my early days with a fly rod. You might say that I felt like I had caught every fish within striking distance of Denver more than once.

One could look at moving away from the Rocky Mountains as the loss of more trout streams than one could fish in a lifetime, but I chose to look at our move to eastern Washington as an opportunity. The little wine town of Walla Walla isn't thought of as a fly fishing Mecca by anyone. Still, there were lots of rivers around, big and small, and just about all of them had runs of steelhead.

They were the fish of legend; impossibly large rainbow trout that could (supposedly) be caught on flies. The steelhead I had seen on the covers of fishing magazines made the trout I was used to catching in my favorite Rocky Mountain trout streams look like bait. If they could be taken on flies, I had to try it.

Despite my renewed motivation to fish; I found myself quite busy with settling in to a new life with my family. It ended up being early 2007 when I finally had the chance to get out and try fly fishing for steelhead.

The dead of winter in eastern Washington is... well, it's cold. Perhaps not the best time to fly fish for steelhead (or anything else, for that matter). The fish can be lethargic in the chilly temperatures. Nevertheless, I tried several rivers, including making the three hour drive to swing flies on the highly acclaimed Grande Ronde River, but didn't hook a single thing. So went the entire season.

Catching fish had long since become the norm in my world, and in good numbers more often than not, and so the idea of multiple fishless outings was a bit difficult to get used to. I hadn't struck out that many times in a row since my days as a new initiate to fly fishing.

Whether you're used to it or not, an unbroken chain of skunkings like that can leave you with a number of questions. Questions like: Do steelhead exist? If you can be satisfied that they exist based on evidence aside from actually catching one, then you naturally move on to the next question: Is the rumor that steelhead will take a fly just an elaborate practical joke, akin to the proverbial snipe hunt?

The times when I could go out fishing every week were long gone. I had a family, and when you have young children, the few days that you can slip away on your own to get in some fly fishing take on a whole new level of value. Spending them catching a whole lot of nothing can leave you wondering if there isn't something more productive you could do with your time. All of these things went through my mind during that first winter of steelheading.

A ray of hope kept me from abandoning the project, just in time for me to have to wait until the next fall to do anything about it. It was my last day out for the season, and I had pretty well decided that steelhead would not take a fly for any reason. I just happened to run across another fly fisherman on a little eastern Washington stream, and he was busy landing a steelhead as I walked up.

It was a healthy buck of around six pounds. It looked like a larger, more athletic version of the rainbows that I was used to, with a trouty pink stripe down its' flanks and some green showing on its' back. It was beautiful, and at that point I would have traded a year of my life for just one fish like that. There was something about the setting, a tiny stream in a dry corner of eastern Washington, four hundred miles from the ocean that made the presence of steelhead seem so unlikely. How could it be there? This was a salt-water fish. It was also a rainbow trout of a size that would make your season on any river in the Rockies. That stream looked like it would only hold moderate-sized trout at best. The whole idea had me virtually salivating over that fish.

In that situation he probably could have told me that the fly I needed was a caddis emerger tied from the nose hairs of a Guatemalan fruit bat and I might have believed him. I needed something to give me some hope and some confidence. The fly he recommended wasn't quite as eccentric as the Nose Hair Caddis. It looked like a pink grizzly-hackle wolly-bugger. He swore it made a difference, and I guess that was good enough for me. He was a very nice guy and offered to give me one, but the day was pretty much over. I thanked him and went on my way, already scheming about next season.

The move to Walla Walla came with a career change for me. I was learning to make wine for a living rather than selling it, and fall was the busiest time of year. Getting out to fish for steelhead at the prime time was going to be difficult, if not impossible, but I would be ready if the opportunity came, with a fly box full of custom tied pink wolly-buggers. I even had a weighted and an un-weighted version. Not the most exciting fly to be sure, but it's not always the glamorous fly that gets the job done. I would target the streams closest to home; the Walla Walla, the Touchet, and the Tucannon; three little tributaries of the Columbia or the Snake that are all about the size of a Rocky Mountain trout stream. I figured I could make that work to my advantage.

The landscape in this part of eastern Washington is mainly rolling hills, often covered with wheat fields as far as the eye can see. In the spring they sway in the wind and waves ripple through them like an ocean of green. In the fall the stubble is a lifeless tan, and when combined with gray skies it can seem a bit bleak, until you develop a taste for it.

The streams that wind through these hills are shrouded in brush and deciduous trees, making them easy to pick out in a landscape where trees are otherwise scarce. Weeds seem to love this part of the world, and making your way to a stream often means fighting through different varieties of thistles as tall as a grown man. Casting can be a bit challenging with heavy cover lining the rivers, and often overhanging branches make it nearly impossible.

While the standing trees can get in the way of casting, the fallen ones make life even more difficult. Most of the time you can't go very far on one of these streams before you come to a fallen tree in the river. If steelhead were really the runners that their reputation suggested, then I figured this could be a problem.

It was late October of 2007 when I managed to get out to the Tucannon again. The river was a place in transition. Green-leafed trees that had not yet given in to the call of the season were interspersed with oranges and yellows, and alongside those were patches of leafless skeletons, foreshadowing the fate they would all soon share. Most of the riverside weeds had died off, leaving their tall, brown husks to guard the place from invading anglers. The sun was out but the air was cool and crisp; it was the kind of day that only comes along in autumn; the kind of day that you might spend wishing you could be out on the river were you not already there.

I didn't know the river well enough to put together the perfect strategy for fishing it, so I ended up just picking a spot and walking in. I fished the place like a trout stream, working my way upstream throughout the morning, which passed without any steelhead, though a couple of trout took my pink fly. That was encouraging, anyway. Afternoons go by quickly at that time of year, and shadows begin to appear on the river soon after mid-day. I didn't have a whole lot of time left.

Having made my way back to my starting point, I began the afternoon walking downstream, looking for spots that were likely to hold fish. Of course, there was a good looking pool not more than twenty yards from where I had come in, hidden by a sharp turn in the river. Apparently I should have gone the other way. No matter, there was still time to fish. There was a fallen log near the head of the run, but the lower part below the log still looked good, with forty yards of open stream before the next set of fallen trees. That was a reasonable amount of space to play a fish on this river, and the hole looked like it had several lies in which a fish could park itself. Behind me was a patch of six-foot-tall bull thistles, but a good deal of space before there were any trees. I could cast normally as long as I remembered to keep my back cast high.

I covered the water close to me with a few short casts from my old six-weight, and then drifted my fly through the center of the run. I had my eye on the far side, where it looked like there was a trough that would make the perfect holding spot for a fish. I landed my fly a few feet above the trough and let it drift down naturally. The line stopped right where I expected the fish to be. I set the hook…

A fish!!! Snags don't thrash their heads when they get hooked, I actually had one!

I paused for a moment, holding tight to the fish as I waited to see what it was going to do. It was slowly dropping back in the current, thrashing and shaking its' head against the unseen force that was trying to pull it out of the water. I had the opportunity to take control of the fight, and I quickly reeled in my slack line so that I could play him on the reel.

The head shakes were powerful, I was pretty sure this was the real deal. I checked my surroundings again, looking for the best place to land the fish. There wasn't much room for error, if he got up a head of steam going downstream in the current below the hole he would make it to the next horrendous mass of fallen trees and that would be it. Most of the pool was shallow and clear, and as he emerged from the trough where he had been holding I caught a glimpse of the crimson stripe on his side.

"Steelhead…" I said under my breath.

Maybe somewhere a starting gun went off, or maybe he saw me the moment I saw him, but all of a sudden the fish turned and bolted downstream. I had no choice but to put the brakes on pretty quickly. If I couldn't turn his head around he would be gone. I would get used to this kind of battle in years to come, and it can definitely go either way; but it's very different from an area where you can let the steelhead go on a long run.

I managed to convince him that going downstream wasn't the thing to do, and the fight unfolded in the heart of the pool. I held my breath as he launched himself into the air, thrashing and spinning as he came down. I was on adrenaline overload; my heart pounding as I leaned on him as much as I dared.

"Don't lose him… don't lose him… don't lose him." I was muttering to myself.

He would be the reward of all of my effort if I could get him in, or a heartbreaking defeat if he got off. I had worked too hard to have it end in defeat…

I played him carefully, and far more nervously than any one fish would normally demand. When the fight was finally over and I knew I had him beat I eased him in to the soft current on the side of the pool and slipped my net under him. He was a hatchery buck that measured twenty-five inches, and weighed in around five to six pounds. He was still in good condition, but very colorful, with a deep crimson stripe dominating his flanks. His back was green, but not dark, and his belly had an orange tint to it that was more reminiscent of a brown trout.

There was something about his colors that seemed in perfect harmony with the season. He looked like fall; fitting into the equation of the season as naturally as falling leaves or harvest festivals. I was smiling ear to ear. If you shout "wha-hoo" in the woods and no one is around to hear it, are you still a dork? Only once before had I ever worked so hard for one fish, and I think I reacted the same way to that one. The feeling of satisfaction certainly reminded me of the day many years earlier when I caught my first big trout on a fly rod.

A six pound hatchery fish is about the average for that system; hardly a huge steelhead, but it is a big trout by anyone's standard. I was amazed at how strong he was. Everything I had heard about the amount of fight in a steelhead was true. I was in the middle of nowhere on a little tributary stream hundreds of miles from the ocean; and there he was, still strong, still determined to reach his goal. No one had caught and released him earlier that day, or yesterday, or the day before that. In all likelihood he had never been hooked before.

I kept fishing for the rest of the afternoon without hooking anything else, but I didn't care. I had finally taken a steelhead on the fly. Everything that I got from fly fishing when I was first learning it; the challenge, the mystery, the anticipation, and the moment when quiet, focused concentration turns into adrenaline fueled excitement in the blink of an eye; it was all restored and then some. A Rocky Mountain trout fisherman was born again that day as a steelheader.

They say that steelhead will find the same lies in a river year after year, generation after generation; so that your grandchildren may well catch fish in the exact same spot that you did decades earlier. The Tucannon's steelhead must have gotten into my head, because ever since that first day in the fall of 2007 they return at the same time each year, finning in the same quiet pool in my imagination, just outside of the main current; drawing me back, defining the season. As difficult as it was for me to slip away to the river at harvest time during my years in Walla Walla, autumn wouldn't have been the same without the Tucannon and its small but feisty steelhead any more than it would be without turkey or football.

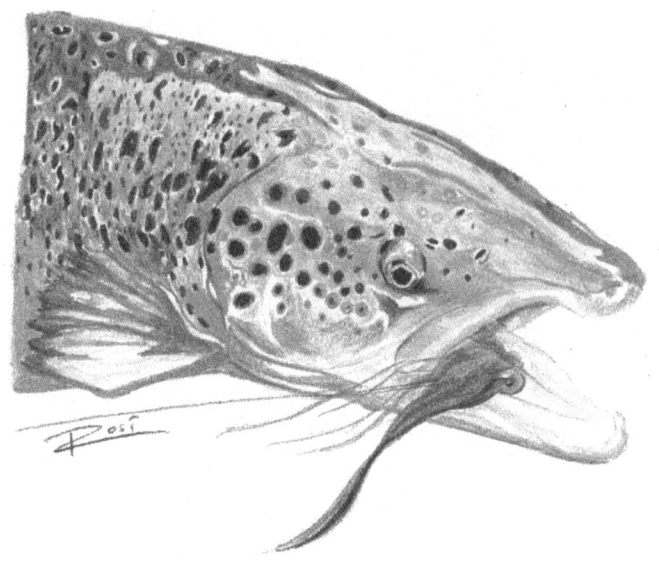

## Suicide Weasels

Tierra del Fuego; Patagonia; Kamchatka; images of these (and other far-away places) bombard the modern angler should he choose to open a fly fishing magazine or wander into a fly shop. Sometimes it seems like the modern fly shop is more like a travel agency that sells a few rods on the side. Wherever you look, you see the same message; the best fishing left in the world is one hell of a long way away from *you,* and if you're even remotely serious about the sport, you'll get your butt on a plane and get after it. Otherwise, well, you just suck.

I guess this new paradigm snuck up on me. I fished quite a bit in my twenties (the 1990s), mostly in and around the Rocky Mountains. I was happy spending the better part of a decade directing nearly all of my angling efforts towards the pursuit of trout with a fly rod, and doing it almost exclusively within a day's drive of home. There was so much territory to explore that I never spent all that much time dreaming of exotic locations (unless Montana can be considered exotic from the perspective of Colorado). It was all right outside my door. Well, metaphorically speaking, anyway. What was actually right outside my door was a typical neighborhood in a suburb of Denver. Still, every year the sport seemed to be more and more about the far-away places where the fishing was still epic in virtually pre-historic proportions.

It wasn't like I was totally immune to the allure of it all, but by the time I became a dad, and fishing took a step down on my ladder of priorities, I was still dreaming about all of the Rocky Mountain trout streams I hadn't gotten to yet. Perhaps that seems a bit sad in the era of the globe-trotting angler who has checked off his entire bucket list by the age of twenty-three, but I guess I never saw it that way.

Don't get me wrong; I had some trips I planned to do "someday". God forbid that I die still languishing in the pitiful backwater bog of non-self-actualized anglers who never managed to fish the entire freakin' world and catch every species in existence with a fly rod. Maybe I'll go to Scotland and keep fishing until I catch a plesiosaur on a dry fly; then I can die happy. Of course, I sort of assumed that my someday would end up being similar to a whole lot of other people; as in, after the kids are grown, and the house is paid off, and I'm retired, and blah, blah, blah.

Maybe it would be different if I could get my own fly fishing T.V. show, but nobody called me to see if I wanted to host *Fly Fishing the World* when John Barrett stepped down. Speaking of which, that's a perfect example of what I'm talking about. You can't just be a trout fisherman anymore. Trout are boring. If you want to impress anyone these days, your quarry needs to be something that is capable of... eating you. Well, we'll see how impressive a Mako shark looks after I land Nessie on a six-weight.

Knowing all that, I suppose it might have looked a tad suspicious to my wife (if she were the suspicious type, that is) that, when I decided to work a vintage abroad as the final step in my education in winemaking, I arranged to do so in a land once described as "The Angler's El Dorado". I mean, would I really go to the trouble of changing careers and going back to school for a couple of years all as a pretense to get to New Zealand?

It wasn't all about fishing. No, really. I love New Zealand wines. It was a great opportunity, and surprisingly easy to arrange.

When I had made the decision to go I gave my twin brother Chris a call to let him know of my plans. He was intrigued...

"Of course I'm going to bring a couple of fly rods along. Who knows if I'll ever get to New Zealand again? I think I'm going to head out a few days early so I can make sure to get some fishing in." I mentioned as casually as I could manage.

That was all he needed to hear.

"You know, I could head out there with you, and we could get a guide and really do it right." He offered.

The ball was rolling.

## Lake Taupo

It was early March of 2008 when we boarded the largest jet I had ever seen for the thirteen hour overnight flight to Auckland. I wish I could say I slept through it, but among my arsenal of supernatural abilities, which can all be categorized as being somewhere between mildly annoying and mostly useless to downright inconvenient, is the ability to lay in bed staring wide awake at the ceiling (any ceiling) when any normal, sane person would have collapsed from exhaustion. So, sleeping on a plane is right out.

We arranged to take a rental car from there down to Lake Taupo, the first stop on our fishing itinerary, for the sake of taking in some of the countryside. It wasn't a terribly long trip, but I must admit that I found driving on the left side of the road to be more disconcerting than I expected, though not so much so as riding as a passenger in the left front seat. I found that in place of a steering wheel, that seat seemed to come equipped with a sense of constant impending doom. Chris felt the same. When I was driving, he let me know that I was about to kill us every thirty seconds or so, and I did him the same courtesy when his turn to drive came up. Of course, I don't recall him falling asleep on the plane either, so…

We met up with our guide that evening in the town of Taupo, which sits on the northeast corner of the lake, to touch base and plan out the next day's fishing. He was a young guy, actually American by birth, who went by the handle of "Fishy Steve". At some point he had decided that the life of a New Zealand fishing guide was the way to go, and he had been at it long enough to have started taking on just a hint of a Kiwi accent. I think he was on to something. I'm already trying to work several different lives into one lifetime, so I guess I'll never know, or at least not first-hand.

Early the next morning we set out, following Fishy Steve to our first destination, the Tauranga-Taupo River. Early March would equate to late summer / early fall in New Zealand, and the weather had been a little drizzly. We made our way up to the middle stretches of the river, which was a small-to-medium sized trout stream. The area wasn't terribly mountainous, but the scenery was more than satisfying in ways that were both familiar and at the same time exotic. In place of the cottonwoods or pines that line many of my favorite streams back home were a variety of interesting native trees, both evergreen and deciduous, including the ubiquitous Southern Beech.

Adding to the somewhat otherworldly, or even primeval feel of the place was what I could only describe as the tallest grass I've ever seen. It grew in patches along the banks of the river, and I later learned that the locals call it Toetoe. It reminded me of Pampas grass (both of them look like Johnsongrass on steroids); with a bushy base of long, slender blades of grass that sends up stalks with whitish, droopy flowering heads reaching heights of up to three *meters*. I guess there's just something about looking up three feet at grass that gets you wondering if there's a population of five-ton ants living nearby.

There was no hatch to speak of, so we proceeded with a nymphing strategy. The stream gave up a few trout pretty quickly. They were good-looking rainbows, mostly about seventeen inches in length. We each caught a few in the first pool, and then spent the rest of the day picking up a fish here and there as we moved around on the river. It wasn't gangbusters fishing, but decent nevertheless.

The way we understood the fishing to break down between the two islands was that the North Island, particularly around Lake Taupo, was reputed to be a good place to go and catch numbers of rainbows. That's not to say that there aren't plenty of big fish around, but based on what we had heard, the South Island was the place to go to stalk big, wily brown trout. In any case, we had come to fish with the idea of catching rainbows, and hopefully good numbers of them.

Our first day of guided fishing wrapped up around the time of the end of a normal work day, leaving plenty of time for a feast; an opportunity that my brother and I are not the type to miss. Fishy Steve had set us up to spend the night in one of the cabins at Kereru Lodge, which sits in a cozy fifteen acre clearing in the woods right on the Tauranga-Taupo. We picked up some steaks for the occasion, and a nice bottle of Merlot from a sub district of the Hawkes Bay region (called Gimblett Gravels) that we were told could produce some interesting Bordeaux style wines. For those not initiated into the world of wine, New Zealand is known primarily for Pinot Noir and Sauvignon Blanc. My brother is a wine guy like myself, and this trip was to include plenty of drinking and tasting. As I recall, this was one of the few times that we drank something other than Pinot Noir on this trip. It was good, but I didn't think it was destined to dethrone Pinot as the king of New Zealand reds.

Put my brother and me next to a river with a drink in our hands and the discussion is likely to wax a bit philosophical; and the topic of why we would go to so much trouble just to go fishing was bound to come up. After all, we could have an experience very much like the one we had just enjoyed without having to go very far at all. Of course, the only rational explanation would be that it actually isn't just to fish.

Chris and I have had this discussion enough times to make it clear that while we do not have exactly the same perspective on the topic, we aren't too far apart. He would say that fly fishing is the perfect excuse for adventure, with the adventure itself being perhaps more the point than the fishing. At least in the case of a trip such as this, that would be precisely correct. We couldn't have gone much farther from home to fish without actually leaving the planet, and the trout fishing was still trout fishing. I don't necessarily disagree with his idea, but I usually argue that when you have a fly rod in your hand you can find adventure anywhere. Whether it is a new piece of water or a well-known stretch on your home river, it is a different world in and of itself, and one which nearly always offers something new to be learned. (Theory: fly fishing is the source of adventure, distance from home is superfluous).

Our slightly different perspectives are most likely a product of circumstance. When you live near good fly fishing, as I have my whole adult life (not an accident), a home water perspective seems perfectly natural. Chris lives in Santa Cruz, California. Don't get me wrong, Santa Cruz is a very nice place, and I always enjoy visiting there, but as a fly fishing Mecca it leaves something to be desired. As a result, when Chris wants to fish, it pretty well means travel, and he does. He has done a number of "bucket list" type trips (in addition to this one), but doesn't get to just grab a rod and head out the door with the expectation of decent trout fishing within reach of home. For me, the experience of getting to know a river intimately is too close to the heart of the matter to do without. In the end I don't think we really disagree all that much on this topic, and we both wish we could enjoy a little bit more of the kind of fishing life the other one has.

Of course all of that philosophizing got us thinking about the river that was just beyond the trees. It still wasn't dark, and the casual "You want to go back out for a bit?" question that kept popping up in the conversation eventually lead to action, and we suited up and headed back down to the river. We stayed out until we just couldn't see our flies anymore, as has been our habit throughout our fishing lives.

There's just something about fishing at dusk. It's the magic hour; you can't just skip it. This strategy can interfere with your campground festivities; especially if you're fishing in Montana in July, where it stays light out until ten o'clock; but this problem can be accommodated easily enough by staying up until two in the morning. It made sense at the time, anyway. Then again, I suppose it had always made sense. When we were kids, we would stay out playing catch until it was so dark that one more throw was likely to cost someone an eye. Maybe some things never change, or perhaps it's just one more example of how fishing is the perfect way to keep from ever growing up.

Since we brought up the notion of the Mecca of Fly Fishing, it bears mentioning that there are a few rivers in the world that could attempt to claim the title. Our next destination, the Tongariro, is one of them. The place was made legendary by the stories of Zane Grey from the 1920's. I even heard "finest rainbow trout river in the world" thrown around in the discussions of the place. Talk about building up your expectations.

The Tongariro empties into Lake Taupo at its' southern tip. The scenery is similar to the Tauranga-Taupo, which is only seven miles or so to the north, but the river itself is larger. A place with the sort of history that surrounds the Tongariro is bound to have a number of colorfully named pools, and the Tongariro is silly with them; featuring names such as the Admirals Pool, Major Jones Pool, Duchess Pool, and the list goes on and on. Speaking of silly, there's even one out there called the Silly Pool, which begs the question as to whether one of the members of the old Monty Python crew named the place. I would have liked to have checked that one out, if only to see if I might have run into John Cleese or Eric Idle on the river.

The pool where we started was just outside of the town of Turangi, and was known as the "Never Fail". If that's not the best name for a stretch of river on the entire planet, I don't know what is. If someone knows of a river with a "Pool of Infinite Lunkers", perhaps I'll change my mind, but until then… Sadly, I've heard that the river has changed since we were there; and the Never Fail no longer appears on the maps, but it was located between the Kamahi Pool and the Hydro Pool.

The Never Fail was nothing short of a piscatorial buffet line. The riffle was wide and perfect, and fed into the pool below at an angle of around forty degrees. The pool was moderately deep, and ran sixty or seventy yards. The trout were everywhere. There was so much perfect water, it was almost too easy. Cast into the riffle, let it drift down into the pool, and there's a fish. Okay, it wasn't like that on every cast. There were some fish in the riffle as well, and sometimes they would grab your fly before it got to the drop-off, so…

We spent most of the morning clobbering very nice rainbows on nymphs. Everything we caught that morning was between sixteen and twenty-one inches and very brightly colored, with green backs and profound red stripes. When it came to producing numbers, the river was living up to its' reputation.

After a streamside lunch we decided to try some other parts of the river with the idea of possibly looking for a few of the bigger fish. We hopped around on a section of the Tongariro that was comparatively narrow and deep, in many places with a steep bank and quick drop-off that made wading impossible. We found ourselves sitting on small cliffs ten or fifteen feet above the water, roll casting to trout holding in deep, clear pools. This strategy produced a few thick, healthy rainbows in the eighteen inch range. Catching fish while seated is a feat normally reserved for bait fishermen, but Chris managed to do just that with a fly rod on the Tongariro.

So ended our day on the world's greatest trout stream. We didn't catch The Trout That Time Forgot, but I think we might have seen it. There were fish holding in impossible to reach spots that looked like they were the size of small submarines. They appeared to be well beyond the ten pound mark, but there was no way to place a cast anywhere near them. Oh well. I'll let someone else decide if the Tongariro really is the greatest. We had a good time fishing it either way.

## Otago

Our next stop was Queenstown, which would be our base of operations for exploring the Central Otago wine region. Touring wine regions was to be as much a part of this trip as fishing, as we are both not only cork dorks in a general sense, but also serious Pinot Noir fanatics. We would stay in Queenstown for a few days, most of which would be devoted to wine, but we figured to take one day and go fishing on our own.

Central Otago is one of the regions (arguably the best) of New Zealand with a reputation for producing world class Pinot Noir. For those who have not yet become familiar with this, the most aromatic of red wines, I can only recommend that you give them a try. A great Pinot can take on the aromas of bright red fruits such as cherries or strawberries, or show dark fruits like plums or blackberries. You might even encounter some that remind you of cola or chocolate; or even earthy, forest floor elements that combine with the fruit aromas to create a complex, multi-faceted wine that has to be experienced to be fully appreciated. One can only describe so much. They can range from light to medium bodied, and there are even a few quasi-full bodied examples out there, though if you are looking for Cabernet-like body, then you should probably look elsewhere. The good ones are silky smooth and match well with a vast array of foods, though for a fisherman, there is nothing quite like a nice piece of salmon and a glass of Pinot Noir. Great Pinot Noirs often come from parts of the world where the question of ripening balances on the edge of a knife, such as here, near the bottom of the world.

New Zealand is also known for Sauvignon Blanc, though perhaps it is the Marlborough region that gets the most attention for this varietal. There was one surprise that we discovered among the wines of New Zealand, and that was the quality of many of the Rieslings being produced. I say it was a surprise not because it doesn't make sense, but just because I really wasn't aware of it. I tasted quite possibly the best New World Rieslings I have ever had while touring the wine regions of New Zealand.

Now if you are automatically thinking of cloyingly sweet, lifeless, uninteresting wine when I say Riesling, allow me to explain that a great Riesling has nothing in common with these cheap imitations. Yes, there are great Rieslings that are made in a dessert wine style that are hyper-sweet, but these are very expensive to produce and also have nothing in common with a $6 bottle from California. The hallmark of a great Riesling, at least if you are speaking of a table wine (rather than a dessert wine) is that, regardless of where it falls on the scale of sweet to dry (yes, there are dry versions), a great Riesling is a perfect balance of sweetness / fruitiness and acidity. Rieslings can offer an array of complex flavors, including a variety of fruits from limes to peaches to melons; stony, sometimes flinty minerality, and (if you have a good one) that refreshing zing of acidity. The aromas of a great Riesling can keep you with a glass to your nose, happily sniffing away for an entire evening.

We had more guided fishing lined up in a few days at the northern tip of the South Island, but we wanted to try our hand at finding some fish near Queenstown on our own. Of course, we wanted to take a shot at stalking big brown trout, and a little research on where we might go to do that lead us to the Mataura River. So off we went in search of big fish. We stopped in at a fly shop around the town of Gore and tried to pick up as much advice as we could and a few local fly patterns, then began exploring the river, looking for fishy spots.

The first stretch of river we tried looked promising enough, but we didn't see any fish. I don't generally expect to be able to see trout in order to be confident that they are around, but when the water is so perfectly clear that you can make out every detail of the riverbed, it can lead you to question just how much time you should devote to casting to fish that clearly aren't there. No matter. We had a few other spots to try.

I rarely go fishing without bringing along my trusty old Orvis tackle bag. It's typically loaded with such an arsenal of tools and gadgets that

MacGyver himself would likely be impressed by the utility of its contents (and could probably improvise a nuclear device from its treasures). On the rare occasion that I go through it, there's always a "Wow, I forgot that was in there..." moment or two. It's even handier when plane travel is involved, as it makes the perfect carry-on. It is endowed with a gazillion pockets and compartments, and it comes pre-packed with all of my favorite fly reels. It allows me to keep my most precious items from being checked and possibly ending up in Tibet. Of course, before taking it on a plane, it must be stripped of anything liquid or pointy. No problem. Most of our fishing was going to be done with guides anyway. They would have all the gadgets we needed. I could leave some of the arsenal at home and travel light; what could go wrong?

Apparently I had forgotten all of the Immutable Laws that Govern the Universe (and fishing trips). As we were re-rigging for our afternoon session, Chris ended up with the business end of a size-ten flying beetle (one of the patterns that we picked up in Gore) lodged in his thumb. Of course the barb was still intact, would this be worth mentioning otherwise? Nevertheless, it's still a rather simple (if somewhat more painful) affair to remove a barbed hook by simply pushing the point of the hook through and clipping the barbed end off with wire cutters. Oh yeah, I took those out. Pinching the barb down was out. We couldn't push it far enough through to get it done. So, there was the hard way (spin the little sucker until it makes a big enough hole that it will come out), the really hard way (rip it out by force), or the really, really hard way (gnaw the thumb off like a coyote caught in a trap).

Or we could go find a set of wire cutters somewhere close by. It seemed reasonable enough. But then, a streamside hardware store within easy striking distance on such an occasion would violate the principles of Murphy's Law to such an extent as to rip the fabric of existence to pieces, and so an hour of potential fishing time was sacrificed to whatever pagan deity regulates fishing trip mishaps (Loki?).

Back at the river, we wandered the banks searching until we finally spotted a big brown trout holding in plain sight. At last, we would have our chance! It was bright and sunny out, and the approach toward the fish was a broad gravel bar that offered no cover at all. The fish went down at the first *move* we made toward it, to say nothing of the first cast, which was utterly futile. They were at least as skittish as we had heard.

We found some deep, dark runs where no trout were visible (nor was the bottom of the river) where it seemed like more familiar tactics might be likely to work. I spent fifteen or twenty minutes casting to a perfect looking cut bank that ought to hold a brown trout in any river from Montana to Pakistan. Eventually I got frustrated and, wondering if all of the browns in New Zealand just held in low, perfectly clear water where they can see you coming from a mile away (rather than a more rational ambush spot like this one), I waded in closer to take a look and see if I could see any fish. I spooked at least three, and one of them looked like it was about as thick as a grown man's thigh. My only consolation was that I had covered the water pretty thoroughly before I spooked the hole.

It looked like the day would end that way until we stumbled across a strange pool on our way out. The fish here (there were several of them) didn't seem spooked by our presence. The sight was downright surreal; like a koi pond full of wild brown trout. We took turns working the different parts of the pool, and while the fish didn't bolt, they showed no interest in our flies, whether dries or nymphs. It was evening by then, and we continued this routine until it was nearly dark; putting one fly after another right in front of the fish and watching them ignore it, or even calmly shift to one side to avoid it.

It was almost dark when I noticed that I had the sort of "wind knot" in my leader that can only be achieved by continuing to cast after you already have tangle. All I could do was cut off everything and call it a night.

"I'm done" I called out to Chris.

Just then, one of the fish came to life. It started coming up and picking off dry flies from the surface. It was moving steadily upstream with each rise, coming in my direction. Chris was following it, trying to place the perfect cast to get a fly in front of a fish that wouldn't hold still. Of course I didn't have a fly at that point, so all I could do was watch with some measure of disbelief as the scene played itself out. After all, every fish in the pool had already rejected every fly we had in our boxes... more than once. Now, out of nowhere, this one fish decided to act like an ordinary trout and start casually feeding on the surface at dusk, and didn't seem to care that we were right there, trying to catch it with phony food. All it took was a well-placed cast and the fish rose to the fly without hesitation. Chris was tied in to what looked like a pretty decent New Zealand brown.

The fish made its' play within the confines of the pool, sparing us from a blind chase downstream. The battle was a tense one, as this was the first big brown either of us had touched on our trip; and of course, in our fervor to tempt the particularly discourteous koi-trout we had resorted to shrinking our flies and tippets to the smallest and lightest available.

The last of the daylight faded as the final moments of the struggle unfolded, leaving Chris to attempt to net the thing in the dark. The big fish / light tippet scenario was hardly an unfamiliar one, but even with experience a lot can go wrong. An errant house fly can crash into 7X and snap it. God forbid the fish bolts right between your legs as you're attempting to net it, leaving you fishless and looking like Inspector Clouseau in the process.

When it looked like the fish was ready, Chris slowly slipped the net under him, lifted, and... No! It jumped clear!

The tippet held, and after the frightened trout had made a couple of laps around the pool, Chris moved in again. This time it went halfway into the net, but the fish was just a little too big. Another thrash and it was swimming again. Miraculously, it was still on the line.

We both knew this couldn't go on forever. One more try was likely to be all he would get.

The net came up around the fish's head, then the rest of it, though I thought that old trout net might break when he lifted the thing.

It turned out to be a nicely proportioned twenty-three inch brown trout that probably weighed in around five pounds. Not a giant by New Zealand standards, but a darn nice fish.

"It's Miller time." Someone observed.

"I don't recall seeing a Miller Central Otago Pinot Noir back at the wine store." Came the reply.

"Well, no, neither do I; but there was one called Soultaker."

"Right. I guess we'll try that one, then…"

## South Island Road Trip

The plan for the next leg of the journey was to drive from Queenstown over to the west coast, then up the coast all the way to the north end of the Island, where we would meet our guide for the trip into the Nelson Lakes region. This was the part where we deliberately stuck ourselves with a drive that was supposed to take around eleven hours for the sake of seeing as much of the landscape as possible. It took longer than we thought, perhaps because we stopped several times, either to eat or to get a better look at some of the more interesting landscapes along the way.

The geography of New Zealand is outrageous. The area around Queenstown has some of the most extreme, jagged mountain ranges I've ever seen. Turquoise lakes and gin clear rivers seem to be around every corner. If you noticed the almost other-worldly backgrounds while watching the *Lord of the Rings* movies, then you have at least some sense of what the terrain looks like; though the true population of elves, orcs, and trolls is substantially lower than one would conclude from the movies. Anyway, at least as long as it was light out, it seemed like driving was the right decision.

I'm not sure at what point roadkill becomes a worthwhile topic of conversation. Or maybe I should say that I'm the one person who is sure, and it's when it seems very much like you must be driving through some sort of death camp for little furry creatures. We'd noticed them before on our initial drive south from Auckland to Lake Taupo, but now, as we were winding our way north through the mountains in route to the Nelson Lakes region, it seemed like they were everywhere. We couldn't identify them, or at least not from the vantage point of a car passing by at highway speed. They were a generic sort of greyish-brown color, about the size of a raccoon, and had bushy tails. That was about all we could make out.

"What's with all the roadkill? I've never seen anything like it." Someone finally said.

"Neither have I. A plague, perhaps?"

"Those usually involve frogs or locusts, don't they?"

"I suppose. So what the hell are those things?"

"I can't tell. They look a bit raccoon-ish, but there are no stripes on the tail."

"They certainly seem to have a talent for getting themselves killed. Does getting run over qualify as natural selection?"

"Only if a few are bright enough to survive. Otherwise it's a self-imposed extinction."

"Maybe it's a local variety of lemming."

"Possibly. But how do we know their deaths are accidental? I mean, just look at all of these things. Besides, they look more like weasels."

"A self-loathing species of weasel with an instinctive death wish?"

"Something like that."

"So, what are you saying? They're offing themselves, is that it?"

"Isn't it obvious? Just how stupid could this species be? So, they're sitting around talking and one says:

*"Hey, where's Bob?"*

And his buddy says: *"Bob's dead."*

*"What about Chuck?"*

*"He's dead too."*

*"Larry?"*

*"Dead."*

*"How are we gonna play poker if everyone's dead?"*

*"I don't know. Hang on, I'm going out into the road."*

*SPLAT.*

*"Hey Ralph."*

*"Yeah?"*

*"Uh, Joey's dead now too."*

*"Oh come on! I need to figure this out. I think I'll go out in the road and..."*

*SPLAT.*

*"Hey guys?"*

*"Yeah?"*

"Have you ever noticed that anytime somebody goes out into the road, they get killed? Maybe we should stay away from the road."

"What? We've always gone into the road. We love going into the road, it's our thing. You're nuts. It's perfectly safe. Watch, I'll show you…"

SPLAT.

"I'm not buying it. Even the most moronic creatures to have ever lived would figure it out eventually. They have to be killing themselves."

"Not necessarily. What if there are so many of them that they spill out into the road by sheer force of overpopulation? See, there's five dead ones together right there. What's that, a mass suicide?"

"Yep."

"So, what are we talking about here? These things sit by the highway waiting for a car to come by so they can hurtle themselves into its' path and go out in a blaze of glory?"

"Exactly. Extra style points are awarded if they get a running start and let out a James Hetfield style 'Yeah!' as they launch themselves into the grill of an oncoming car…"

"Of course. It's all perfectly clear now. So, what if one were to, say, complete a full-twisting laid-out Tsukahara right into the business end of a speeding vehicle?"

"I suppose they would make it their King, wouldn't they?"

"Well yes, I suppose so; posthumously, anyway."

"That goes without saying."

"King of?…"

"The Suicide Weasels."

"Right."

A good portion of the evening was spent speculating about the nature of the oddly anthropomorphic little Suicide Weasel and its' most peculiar set of habits. By the time we were done, the New Zealand Suicide Weasel was a particularly intriguing, dare I say even endearing little species. After all that I guess I couldn't help going back and investigating when I had the chance. When I did, I discovered that our furry little friends were actually brushtail possums (a creature vastly less interesting in every way than the Suicide Weasel). They were introduced to New Zealand by Europeans with the idea of creating a fur industry. Since there are no large predators around to eat them, they have become a nuisance, and no one minds that they are dying on the roads in droves. Apparently they are enough of a problem that the place would be better off if they could be eradicated completely. The thought that the little bushy-tailed beasties might be possums never occurred to me, as my idea of a possum is a creature that looks like a hideous giant rat with a distinctively hairless tail. So much for our satisfaction from having named a new species.

## Nelson Lakes

The pinnacle of our trip had arrived. We were headed for Nelson Lakes National Park, for a hike in trip to a river that I have agreed not to name in print. We'll call it River X. There are several things to know about the fishing in this part of New Zealand. For one, the big fish often are found by employing the opposite strategy from what you might use in the U.S. Certainly it is often true anywhere that better fishing can be found by going upstream and deep into remote areas, but here instead of perhaps finding a population of fish that are more plentiful and more willing to take a fly (and smaller), you often find the biggest fish in the system.

Having read about this, we arranged a trip to hike in to a spot that was considered pretty remote. There were no roads that would allow access to River X at all. Even the trail head was inaccessible. We had to hire someone to take us by boat just to get to it. Mike Kirkpatrick, our guide for this grand adventure, had asked us if we were in shape for a three hour hike, and we had told him that we could do it. We were both thirty-seven at the time, and we both did at least some exercise. Personally I figured that if I could survive working a harvest at (any) winery (try doing punch-downs on open-top fermenters full of Pinot Noir for twelve hours a day if you want to know what I'm talking about), a three hour hike should be no problem.

The plan was to use one of the huts built along the hiking trail as our base camp, and that was our destination as we began our hike. The back country of New Zealand is littered with these things, as "trekking" (wandering through the countryside for its' own sake) is quite popular with the younger folks, both locals and many who come from Europe for the same purpose. We had to pack everything in, including food and gear, so we were probably encumbered to the tune of fifty pounds or so per person. I hadn't given much thought to what that might mean over the course of three hours, but I wasn't too concerned. The one thing I definitely had not counted on was the trail being anything but (relatively) flat.

My weight can be a bit of a moving target, but the average over my adult life has been around two hundred fifteen pounds, which is admittedly heavy for someone five foot ten. I have kept up some weight training throughout most of my life, and at the very least I can say that the extra weight is not all fat. Chris is about the same size, although he has been more consistent with the working out than I have. He didn't appear to be carrying too much extra weight around the waist at the time. Mike was around our age, but he had to be at least fifty pounds lighter than either of us, and he was moving fast. I could tell pretty quickly that the hike was going to be more challenging than I had planned.

Okay, it was a lot more challenging. The trail was anything but flat. Most of it was scrambling up and down across the side of a mountain, hoping not to lose one's footing and go rolling down into a ravine, bouncing off of trees and rocks on the way down. None of these things were slowing Mike down. I suppose I only have myself to blame, after all, I told him I was in shape for a hike. Next time, I'm going to ask for more specifics.

Also readily apparent was the spectacular beauty of River X and its' surrounding canyon. High snow-capped peaks framed both sides along much of its length, and a full-scale forest of southern beech blanketed the landscape down to the river. Here again was the feeling of a primordial forest; as if at any moment a tyrannosaurus might poke its head out of the trees. As for the water; it was as perfectly gin-clear as any I have ever seen.

Of course, New Zealand has no large predators, or even snakes, much less an actual T-Rex. It's one of the things that makes a wilderness expedition in this part of the world totally different from virtually any other place where one might go to do this. While this is extremely convenient, as you have quite a bit less to worry about, one could argue that something is lost from the experience as a result. After all, doesn't some risk of being eaten create a more "authentic" wilderness experience, or at least a heightened sense of being away from civilization? I mean, if there isn't anything around that might eat you, in a sense you might as well be fishing in the park two blocks from your house.

"Knowing that there are nine-foot-tall Kodiak Bears around that can swat your head clean off and then play with it like a soccer ball keeps things interesting." My brother observed, comparing the trip to his last Alaskan adventure.

Be that as it may, our guide warned us that the most dangerous animal we would encounter in this area was a particularly aggressive (apparently Germanic in origin) species of wasp, that would go after you if you put your hand on the wrong tree.

"That's good to know" I said as one of the little black and yellow demons extracted it's stinger from my arm and went along its merry way. The little monsters don't even have the decency to die afterwards.

My hand was, in fact, on a tree. At least it was a sign that Mike knew what he was talking about. The welt that developed on my forearm itched for weeks.

"Feels like a hot needle, doesn't it?" Mike asked.

"Funny, I was just thinking the same thing...." I replied.

We managed to make it to the cabin, and not too far off schedule. Chris and I both needed some time to re-hydrate and recover from the brutal leg cramps we were experiencing from the hike. Word to the wise: when a New Zealand fly fishing guide asks you if you're in shape for a three hour hike into the back country, be sure to take them seriously.

Another nearly unique thing about this area is that it is safe to drink the water directly from the river without treatment. Thank goodness, otherwise we would have had to pack in several gallons of water. We filled our bottles from the river and gave it a try. In case anyone is wondering what water tastes like from a pristine, unspoiled source like this, all I can say is, well... well... it just tastes like water. Sorry. I just don't get that excited about water. If it tasted like Domaine de la Romanee-Conti from a good vintage maybe I would be more enthused. I guess it didn't taste as much like chlorine as typical tap water if that is makes you feel better.

I was in a spot. My legs were in knots, but there was the river, beckoning me. This was the climax of our trip, a remote river where we would be stalking big brown trout in perfectly clear water. We pulled ourselves together much more quickly than what was actually prudent and got ready to fish.

I said that there are several things to know about fishing in this area. The second is that the browns tend to be relatively solitary, and often you will find one big fish alone in a pool, and it may well be right out in the middle in plain sight. The third is that the trout are every bit the ultra-skittish, spook at the slightest hint of danger, see you coming from a mile away fish that their reputation suggests, particularly late in the season, which it was.

When Mike told us that we would be fishing with leaders up to twenty-five feet long, my first thought was that it was impossible. A leader that long would never straighten out. As it turned out, it was possible. We started with long tapered leaders or polyleaders and built down from there.

*Suicide Weasels*

It wasn't like it was fifteen feet of tippet. There was a lot of tapering going on. Also, the fly line had to be camouflaged. A natural, dull green color was best. The idea was to eliminate anything that might catch the eye of the trout and put it down. Getting close enough to the fish to put a fly in front of it was the most challenging. Staying low or approaching from far behind was just the beginning. Once in the river, one had to move with absolute stealth. A wading boot turning on gravel could be enough to spook a fish. The guide would remain where he could see the fish and the angler would slowly creep into position, then put his cast right where the guide instructed. Conditions dictated nymphs, but, of course, no strike indicators. The first cast could well be your only shot, so it was imperative that it be well placed. The guide would watch for the take, and then yell "Strike!" when it happened.

To keep the weight of our packs down, we had to leave the waders behind. We would be wading wet. March is fall in New Zealand, but the weather appeared to be cooperating, so I wasn't too concerned.

Chris had already taken a pretty nice brown at the Mataura, so we decided that I would be up first. We came to the first pool and Mike went to work. Having one of these guys on your team is like having a good bird dog. They see everything. Now I realize that experience with a river would teach you where to look for fish, but it really did seem like Mike had x-ray vision when it came to spotting trout. There were times when we were standing right next to each other, and I still couldn't see the darn things.

The fish was right in the middle of the pool, which was about three feet deep, thirty feet wide, and featured a walking speed current. Pretty easy to fish, unless, of course, you have to sneak up on the trout without making a sound.

I managed to wade into position without spooking the fish, then cast my fly as close to where I thought Mike wanted it as I could.

"Good cast. That might do it… strike!" Mike said.

I brought my rod up and felt… nothing. I watched two very nice browns swim past my legs in a panic. One looked like it was around eight pounds.

"You didn't feel him? I saw him open his mouth." Mike said.

"Nope. I never had him." I replied.

Who knows what happened. The fish could have taken something right next to my fly. I might have been just a hair late on the hook-set. Regardless, it was the only time that Mike ever called for a hook-set and nothing was there.

There was one more fish in the pool, and we tried a half dozen flies to coax a take out of him, but it never came. An hour of wet wading had changed my outlook on the weather. It may have felt like summer when you were dry, but the breeze carried the unmistakable chill of fall, and I was ready to find a sunny spot to warm up.

Before long we came to a ridge with a steep, brush-lined bank that sloped down to a nice run where Mike spotted our next target. I stayed up high on the ridge above to watch the action from there, while Chris and Mike crept into position. The fish was in plain sight in a section of the river that was neither deep nor broad. The only thing there was to help hide them was the tall grass along the side of the stream. They managed to get into range without spooking the fish, but it refused the first offering, and moved downstream.

Well, crap. After spending an hour at the last hole trying fly after fly without success, it looked like we were now going to be 0 for 2. But we waited to see what the fish would do. It hadn't bolted, just moved slowly away. Chris and Mike followed, keeping some distance to prevent spooking the already wary trout. Twenty yards later it settled in and began feeding once again.

I had just settled in to drip-dry. They were out of my line of sight now, behind the wall of brush along the steep river bank, but they were close. I could still hear Mike whispering:

"There he is. He's feeding again now. Put your cast a couple of feet left of the rock."

I didn't want to go crashing down and inadvertently spook the fish just to get a better view, so I waited, listening for the sound of…

"Strike!" I heard Mike call out.

I jumped up and scrambled down around the patch of brush to see if the fish was on. Chris' rod was bent double, and the fish was headed downstream. We all followed, and watched as the fight played out in moderately-sized riffle. Chris had himself another big brown, this one a well-built, heavily spotted six-pound beauty.

I guess the pressure was on now. I was still waiting for my first. The next fish we spotted was holding in a spot that was a little different; a thigh-deep pool just above a rapid. Standing in the rapid would offer the advantage of covering any noise I made. The disadvantage was that I was *standing in the friggin' rapid.* It wasn't the worst spot I've ever put myself in to make a cast, but the current was heavy enough that a misstep would probably mean going for a swim.

Mike and I got into position, him to see the fish and me to put a cast over it. The fish took the first cast and immediately turned and ran downstream past me through the fast water. We were fishing small nymphs on relatively light tippet, so I had to let it run. I also had to get myself out of the rapid if I wanted to have any chance of landing it.

I turned back toward shore, taking step after careful step as the fish swam away downstream, painfully aware that the cheap rubber-soled wading boots I had picked up just for this trip didn't grip quite like the studded felt that I was accustomed to. My feet seemed to slide with every step I took, but I managed to make my way back to solid ground.

The fish had moved down past the rapid into calmer water, where the fight became a matter of time and side pressure, and I eventually prevailed. It was another very nice brown of five and a half pounds or so. Mike was chuckling as he walked over to offer his hand.

"I wasn't so sure about that one. I gave you maybe a fifty-fifty shot at getting him in. Well done." He said.

"I thought you were gonna pull a Paul Maclean for a second there…" Chris added.

Apparently Chris had been half expecting to see my interpretation of the scene from *A River Runs Through It* (the movie) where Paul (Brad Pitt) hooks a big fish and then ends up floating downstream through heavy rapids to land it. I suppose that would have made for a better (albeit a bit plagiaristic) story. It sure would have made one heck of a You-Tube video. Some of it was caught on film, anyway. I, for one, was happy to have disappointed my audience. Over the years I've had a mishap or two while playing fish; I've even dunked myself and still managed to land the fish, but getting swept downstream in a rapid just doesn't sound like something I want to experience for myself, with or without a trout on the line.

I felt pretty good. I had my brown trout and apparently no one thought I was going to land it. Cool. What's more, all the browns we were catching (all three, anyway) were impressive looking fish.

We continued hunting for fish after that until it got dark, but we didn't get anything more. We headed back to the cabin with a total of one fish apiece.

"It's great that you guys both caught fish the first afternoon. That really takes the pressure off. These things aren't easy to get; you guys did well." Mike observed as we were walking back.

Language is a funny thing; and for speakers of English, which is spoken in so many parts of the world, it seems fascinating to me to observe the little things that make it a bit different wherever you hear it. So, if you were imagining that our guide sounded like a good old boy from the U. S. of A., well, think again. And, if you've never heard a native New Zealander speaking our shared language, you're best off imagining that it sounds more British than American. It's not exactly the same, mind you, but the differences between the pronunciations and inflections of a Kiwi versus a native of the United Kingdom are more subtle than those that separate us from our cousins across the pond. Or at least that was the way it seemed to me.

That is not the case, however, with the short vowel sound of the letter 'e'. On this one, the Kiwis are off on their own. As far as I can tell, this sound does not seem to exist in their version of English. That makes it difficult to manage a "proper" pronunciation of my good Irish first name, and so I took notice right away. It comes out sounding like "Kiv'n". The difference didn't stop there, of course. Eggs were "iggs", left was "lift", and so on. Okay, maybe no one else would care about something like that, but it made for an interesting distinction as far as I was concerned.

New Zealanders also seem to have a particular penchant for contractions. When Mike commented about how we Americans have a tendency to draw out our words, I had no idea of what he meant. I soon figured it out, though, starting with the way everyone there said my name. Then there was the name of the town nearest to the winery where I was to spend the harvest, which I naturally wanted to pronounce phonetically. Blenheim. That seemed clear enough. Not even close. Try "Blin'm" (apparently the British also pronounce it this way, but then they like their contractions as well). So, as far as I can tell, "draw out our words" = "pronounce all of the syllables", and it seems that this is not the convention in other former British colonies, nor is it in the "motherland" either. Does all this mean that we Am'ricans speak English like Germans?

Anyway, I guess Chris and I both took something away from the experience. If someday you find yourself fishing a trout stream in the American west, and you happen to hear someone yell "Strike!" New

Zealand fly fishing guide style ("stroyk"), feel free to come over and say hello. It might be my brother and me spotting fish for each other.

Our fishing hut was comfortable and awfully convenient. It was a fairly plain, rectangular building with a small covered porch and featured a food prep area, wooden bunks that would accommodate up to ten people, and a bench where one could sit and eat. It was set in a meadow situated near the river, but not exactly right on it. New Zealand has quite a few of these backcountry huts, which are maintained by the Department of Conservation, and they are available for use by the public. The cost to use one of them was cheap (kind of like camping back home in the early 90s), and I don't know of many (if any) campgrounds that are maintained that far from any road in the U.S.

As convenient and (relatively) comfortable as the whole set-up was, I didn't sleep much, and was relieved when morning came. The outhouse proved to be a bit of a challenge as well; not that one expects the restrooms in the back country to resemble the Ritz-Carlton, mind you. In fact, one doesn't necessarily expect restrooms at all, so having anything ought to be considered a luxury. This one, however, happened to be home to a small army of those evil wasps. We'd already become acquainted with one another and I'd found them somewhat less than amicable. In fact, the welt on my arm had done nothing but get worse and was itching something awful. The thought of encountering more while using the facilities was enough to get me thinking of hiking back to the civilized world. But then, there were fish to be caught, so…

The little buggers left me alone. Perhaps they have some sense of civility after all. Still, I couldn't help feeling a bit like George Washington, who apparently made a habit of riding into battle at the head of his troops on a big white horse, making a perfect target of himself for the whole world; and always came away unscratched. Protected by God…

We were on our way before sunrise. In the pre-dawn silence even the sound of our feet falling on gravel was like a stampede. The world was still save for us and the river flowing in the background; making it difficult not to feel a bit like an invading army. We walked by starlight toward the river until we reached the line of trees, then even that was gone. The river was shrouded in darkness.

We made our way carefully until the sky began to brighten. A morning mist hung low over the water as the scene revealed itself; the dark, imposing forms that surrounded us becoming green and benevolent once again. Our mission could wait long enough to stop and take it all in.

Experiencing perfect moments in nature can leave you wondering if this isn't the real heart of the matter, and the catching of fish more like a positive externality. Would it be better to simply stand back and absorb it all, to look without touching; or to join the quiet dance of the river; of hatching insects and feeding trout, and water restlessly moving, slowly but surely back to the ocean?

By now I suppose I know my answer. For me, the pull of the fish is too strong. But then we have a role to play in this scene as well, though it is one that can be difficult to define. We are both alpha-predator and trickster, taking our prey not by speed or strength but by deceit, only to release it again in an act that would seem to render the whole endeavor pointless. The trout, after all, do not consume insects only to spit them out again. They have a clarity of purpose that we, or at least most of us, have lost. If we fail to take our quarry we do not fear going hungry, and so the question of "why" seems to haunt us; and the answer "for fun" explains so little.

Do we do this in memory of something we once were? Or is it a connection to something that we still are; underneath all the trappings and conveniences of modern life; a connection that can fade from the vantage point of an office in a skyscraper or a vehicle idling in traffic, and one that can't be quite fully experienced as an onlooker alone? To feel this connection is to know that we are a part of the natural world; not something that exists alongside or even outside of it, but a participant that belongs there every bit as much as a feeding trout or a hatching mayfly. Whether we need the fish for food or not, we are what we are.

Fishing over the same spots that we had hit the day before was unlikely to produce, but we were off to a much earlier start, so we could easily go farther upstream and find some virgin water. We soon came to a pool with a clearing on our side of the water and a fallen log across it. It was a particularly spectacular setting. Crystal clear water ran up against bleached white rocks on the bank. The background of tall streamside grasses and beech trees fell against wooded hillside, leading up to jagged, bare rock mountains with just a sprinkling of snow, all framed by perfectly clear blue skies.

The trout was sitting just in front of the log, a problematic spot. Not so much for the presentation, but, well, you know. Chris and Mike got set up, the cast was made and the fish hooked. Then it got interesting. The fish went for the fallen log, as we all figured it would, which had Mike just a bit concerned.

"Get it away from that tree! Get it away from that tree!" He called out, clearly concerned that we were about to lose the first fish of the day.

Chris seemed less concerned. He had managed to stop the trout's run just before it got under the log.

"I've got him." He said in response.

He continued to lean on the fish until it yielded. Come to think of it, that would have to be a little embarrassing for the fish. "Break Him Off on the Log" is the most sure-fire strategy in the trout playbook, and the log was right there. It must feel kind of like being unable to punch it into the end-zone from one yard out.

New Zealand guides will make it clear to you right off the bat that using side pressure is your best bet against these things, much like steelhead fishing back home. The main difference, it seemed to me, was that they would tell you to try to keep the pressure on the same side of the fish in an effort to wear out the muscles on one side of its body as quickly as possible. This was different from the strategy often used for steelhead, in which you may well change the direction of pressure in order to disorient the fish so that it can't figure out how to fight back effectively.

And so Chris was on the board quickly with another excellent specimen in the net, albeit a tad smaller than the others we had caught. Still, it was another nice looking male brown trout, with fantastic spots and coloration.

Now Chris and I had been wandering the back-woods of New Zealand in our usual fishing attire, blissfully unaware of any possible dire consequences for doing so. What I mean by that is that we were sporting either short-sleeved shirts, or long-sleeved fishing shirts with the sleeves rolled up. Mike had been wearing long sleeves with sun gloves at all times. I didn't think much of it at first. I don't recall anyone warning us that we might encounter mosquitos, and I hadn't seen any. Perhaps he just wanted to avoid sunburn.

Or not. Maybe we had been warned and it just didn't register. I don't recall, but we were both being eaten alive by the most dangerous predator on the island: sand flies. You don't hear them mentioned too much in tourist brochures, or really anywhere else. Strange, that. No one really talks about them at all. Come to think of it, if word gets out that I'm doing so here, I suppose it's possible I might get a visit from a couple of men in black from the New Zealand Department of Tourism.

Anyway, Chris and I were both being harassed by the little monsters and the bites were starting to accumulate (and to itch), particularly on the hands. Unlike mosquitos, these things rip and tear at your flesh to get at your blood, or at least that's the way it was explained to me. Either way, mosquitos are a pleasant companion by comparison. The sand fly bites actually hurt, and the welts hung around and itched (literally) for weeks. Still, I couldn't help thinking about how, in a twisted way, we were actually getting our wish. We were in the back-country, fishing a remote river, and we were being eaten by wild animals. Slowly and very inefficiently perhaps, but nevertheless… eaten.

Of course such things seem inconsequential when one is out after fish. There's plenty of time to scratch itchy bug bites on the plane ride home. We pressed on to the next pool, where Mike spotted a fish that was in shallow water up under a tree.

"That's a tough one." He said.

"You'll need to be directly behind the fish, so you'll have to be under the trees as well. Think you can make that cast?" He asked.

The trees were around eight feet above the surface of the water, so things would have to happen low. False casting would be an invitation to disaster.

"Yeah, I can do this." I told him.

It didn't look so tough to me, not because I'm a champion caster (I'm not), but because I use a water-loaded, back-handed, side-arm flip all the time; generally out of, well you could call it laziness or a desire for efficiency, you choose. Either way, it would work just fine for this situation.

After slowly and painstakingly positioning myself in the river, I peeled (what looked like) just enough line off of my reel, letting it straighten out in the water behind me. I got my bearings, picked a target based on where I thought Mike wanted it, then slowly brought my rod tip forward, lifting it to shoulder-level as I went, allowing the current pulling on the line to load the rod. I quickly flipped it forward, and a nice, tight-looped cast laid out well under the lowest branches of the tree, landing the fly right about where I wanted it. It was only a twenty-foot cast, and I'd done it many times before, but I still felt pretty good about it just then.

Guides can be hard to read sometimes. It was easy to see that Mike wanted to catch fish, and he didn't want to blow opportunities. He was quick with praise when things went properly, and equally quick to scold should you (for example) do anything that might alert a trout to your presence. Maybe he was used to working with people who claimed to be expert casters and then couldn't get it done when they got out on the water; or maybe he had just learned that pumping up a client's ego was a better plan than letting them know that they weren't as good as they thought. One way or another, he was always complimentary when a cast went where it was supposed to go, and it seemed genuine to me.

"Nice cast... strike!" I heard once again.

I set the hook and he was on. He bolted downstream about thirty yards before pausing to froth up the water with a berserking thrash-fest. The tiny hook came free. I knew we weren't likely to land every fish, but I was still a bit crestfallen that I didn't get to see that fish.

We continued upstream until late afternoon, finding a trout here and there as we went. There was one that required that I max out my ability to cast for distance. I couldn't convince that one to take the fly. I managed to hook and lose one more. Chris got one more before the day was out, clearly a once mighty buck that was now spawned out.

Finally, after hiking most of the day, the river began to grow narrow and the terrain steep, until we reached a point where fishing became impossible. It seemed strange that we would keep going, hiking along a boulder-strewn ridge far above the river with no way down. Then we saw it; from atop a forty-foot cliff, we could look down into a blue-green pool set between enormous boulders. It looked deep, at least ten feet, yet the fish that was finning right in the middle was as clear as day. Even from our distant perch we could tell he was a beauty; but there was no way to get near. All we could do was watch, which we did for some time, then began the trek back to the cabin.

The next day we hiked back out along the river, stopping now and then to cast to a fish that our cabin-mates had likely hooked (or at least tried for) the day before, but the trout weren't having it.

The brown trout of the South Island had lived up to their billing; incredibly challenging and equally rewarding. We came away with stories of fish fooled and fish that couldn't be hooked, fish landed and fish lost. Not bad.

## Marlborough

There was no denying that the fishing portion of our trip was winding down. We were on our way to the Marlborough region, in the northern part of the South Island. There I would be working the vintage, and we planned to spend our last few days exploring the wine region, and, of course, tasting some wines.

The geography of the area seemed familiar; a broad valley filled with neatly manicured rows of vines extending nearly as far as the eye can see, climbing partly up the sides of the foothills before forest takes over and true mountains begin. For a couple of days we went from winery to winery, sampling some excellent Sauvignon Blancs, Pinot Noirs and Rieslings (and a few other varietals) and we were generally content to do so. Still, the subject of where to go to squeeze in one more day of fishing kept coming up.

We eventually decided to drive north a bit to a river called the Pelorus, which was supposed to offer pretty good fishing and easy access. Most everyone has probably seen the Pelorus without actually being aware of it; think: a bunch of dwarves and a Hobbit floating in wine barrels. That's right, it's Peter Jackson, once again sharing the spectacular landscapes of New Zealand with the rest of the world in The Hobbit. We were there in 2008, before The Hobbit was made, so it wasn't like we planned our outing around the idea of checking out a location from the movie, but we did get to see some of the canyon stretches while we were prospecting around, looking for a good stretch to fish. We eventually decided on the lower section, where there was less whitewater, access was easier, and there wasn't quite so much of a problem with Orcs (they're bait-fishermen, you know…).

There are a few things that every outdoorsman dreads. No, dammit, not Orcs. They aren't a problem outside of New Zealand, anyway. I guess the greasy fried chicken we wolfed down for lunch before heading out wasn't agreeing with Chris; and any kind of stomach distress while out in the woods can be enough to ruin your day, and can mean calling the whole thing off, regardless of how far you've come to fish. No sooner were we wadered up and ready than we had to head back toward Havelock, the only town anywhere near us, looking for some place that had a restroom and some stomach medication.

That sounded easy enough. All we needed was a gas station or convenience store. Or so we thought. The convenience stores turned out to be nothing like the ones back home, where you could expect to find a selection of just about anything you might need for minor emergencies, from aspirin to radiator fluid. We found nothing on the shelves of the couple of stores that were open that day in Havelock that would help. We inquired as to where we might find basic stomach medications and were told that we would have to go to the chemist (pharmacist), which was (of course) closed that day.

The next town was another hour down the road, and it was already mid-afternoon. It would be pointless to come back after two more hours on the road. It was up to Chris to say whether we were going home or going fishing. We could've found something else to do for the rest of the afternoon, but I can't say I was surprised when he decided to tough it out.

Back at the river, we found an officially designated access point and made our way to the water. A perfect looking gravel bar gave way to a broad run that tapered off gently to the far, deep side, which was nicely shrouded with overhanging trees. The canyon had opened up into a small valley, surrounded by hills and moderate-sized mountains, complete with more native Beech forests. There were a few clouds around, but mostly clear skies, mild temperature, and just a slight breeze. All-in-all, a nice setting for our last day on the water.

When we finally stepped into the river, we were met with the sight of what seemed to be hundreds of rising fish. They were all in the shallow water along the near bank, which would make them easy pickings. Jackpot!

Well, almost. They were all dinks. Now, in general, I have nothing against an afternoon spent catching small fish on dry flies. It's low-pressure, relaxing, easy fun. Still, I'm going to guess that even those who have published stories about the virtue to be found in eschewing high-pressure hog-farm fishing in favor of catching six inch brookies on a two-weight in tiny, remote eastern streams wouldn't be likely to fly to the other side of the world to do so. There was supposed to be some big ones around, and we weren't going to get 'em by flipping dries to a pod of suicidal six-inchers all day. Nevertheless, we continued casting to them in a nearly hypnotic state for what seemed like an hour. Each time I caught 'just one more', another fish would start rising right in front of me.

At some point I shook my head and broke free of the rising fish trance.

"These things are all small. We should start working that far bank and find some bigger fish." I called out.

That was when I found out that Chris' luck that day hadn't improved. He must not have had quite the right fly, because the fish weren't giving him the time of day. I suppose I could have given him one, but he hadn't come to New Zealand to catch dinks either. Daylight was burning.

We went different directions to stake out a hundred yards or so of river to work. I decided to tie on a parachute hopper with a small nymph as a dropper. Not so much because there were hoppers around (I hadn't seen any), but because I figured the fish would take the nymph, and a big, bushy hopper would make a good indicator. And hey, what's better than taking big fish on big flies? It could happen.

Something kept grabbing the nymph and pulling the hopper under. It felt fishy, but nothing was there when I set the hook. Whatever it was, it just didn't quite want to commit. After a few attempts, I finally managed to get the cast just right, landing my hopper up under some overhanging brush where a big trout might want to hide.

"That should do it…" I thought to myself.

The water exploded as a big fish came up and demolished my hopper!

I lifted my rod and the hook set true. All I had to do was get him away from the brush and trees on the far side, and there would be nothing but open water to play him out.

A big rainbow in open water is just plain fun. The runs, the jumps, all without fear of a snag. Sure, they still get free sometimes, but it's all part of the game. I let him have his fun (okay, it was me having all the fun) and then brought him to the net. He was a pretty, twenty-one inch male rainbow.

Things were looking up. We should both be able to get a few more like that before the end of the day; and who knows? Maybe there was a big brown around as well. That would be the perfect way to end the trip.

I'm not sure when the background music started. There was a house up high on the far bank right next to the bridge we had crossed to find our access point. The occupant was *blasting* Ozzy Osbourne loud enough for anyone in the area, including us, to hear. I didn't think much of it at first. Someone was listening to loud music on their deck, no cause for concern. Chris had walked down below the bridge to look for fish in some promising spots, and I was still working the far bank, moving slowly toward the bridge.

As I came into shouting range of the house, someone began screaming obscenities, and apparently I was the target. I couldn't make out everything that was being said (screamed), but among them was:

"Go back home and catch your own (@%*!#!!) fish!"

This guy, apparently the owner of the house beside the bridge, was completely unglued. To say the least I was caught off-guard. What was he so worked up about? We'd done our homework, and we knew this was public water. Hell, the access point was right behind me.

I decided to just keep walking down under the bridge, heading toward where Chris was fishing. We could then continue to cover water throughout the afternoon without getting completely separated. I had no interest in actually engaging this lunatic, preferring to finish out my day of fishing in peace. I would just keep moving and leave him to listen to the sound of his own screams.

It wasn't until much later that I realized that I could have explained to him that the fish we were catching were actually McCloud River (California) Rainbows, and so, in a way, they were my fish. Oh well, one of those "I should've said…" moments. I don't suppose that it would have calmed him down.

When I emerged on the other side, there was the guy again, and this time he started throwing rocks… so much for my plan to ignore him. I couldn't tell if he was aiming for me or if he was just trying to spoil the fishing, but I wasn't going to just wait until he beaned me in the head to be sure.

"Hey!" I shouted back. "What's your problem, man?!" I bent down and found a rock in the river, then cocked my arm so I knew he could see what I was doing. "Go ahead, throw one more!"

He was up on the bridge, a bit of a long throw, but it stopped him for the moment. My mind was racing; I could see the possible outcomes of a confrontation playing out in my imagination like a movie at double fast-forward speed. I had a job lined up that I was supposed to report to in a few days, and it had been no small thing to set all that up. I was in a foreign country, and trouble was the last thing I needed. I really didn't want to have to make a call to my wife to let her know I was in jail on the other side of the world. I made up my mind that I wouldn't engage this guy physically unless I had to.

"I'm gonna go get my gun!" I heard him yell from the bridge.

Chris had heard what was going on by then and was on his way over. We didn't have too much time to decide if we thought he was crazy enough to actually pull out a gun, as he soon reappeared on the bank and started throwing rocks again. He still wasn't coming all that close to hitting me.

Maybe he was just trying to scare us off, or maybe he just grew up playing soccer. As for me, well, I grew up in southern California, where we played baseball year-round, and rock-boy was now well within my range.

I fired a warning shot that whizzed right by his head, hoping that would convince him to back off.

"Throw another one!" I yelled, as I cocked my arm with another rock, trying to decide if I actually wanted to aim for his head.

Fortunately, I never had to decide. He stopped throwing rocks and started coming closer, still shouting obscenities at the top of his lungs. He was virtually foaming at the mouth, screaming incoherently. There was something in there about his "water supply". I couldn't make out much else. Maybe he was pumping river water up to his house, but what did that have to do with us? You wouldn't do something like that without proper filtration in place, so what could we have done to harm his water supply? We hadn't trespassed. We were on public water. We were just fishing and generally minding our own business.

He stopped shy of coming down to the water. He was threatening and egging us on like he now wanted to fight, but he wasn't coming any closer. Was this guy wacked out on hard drugs? It kind of seemed that way, but he was able to choose to not get hit in the head with a rock, so something was still working upstairs.

He couldn't be serious about wanting to fight. He looked like he was in his fifties, around 5'8", and perhaps 165 (saggy) pounds. He wasn't exactly an imposing figure, and he was facing two younger, larger men. The guy sure deserved an ass-whipping, but I became all the more determined that were there to be a fight, I would be standing in the water. He didn't appear to have actually brought a gun, but I really didn't want to find out the hard way that New Zealand had a "Make My Day" law.

Who knows what he expected to happen. Whatever the case was, he probably hadn't counted on the fact that Chris was already having a bad day. He started up the bank, apparently to give the rock-chucker the fight he seemed to be looking for.

"Don't go on his property!" I warned.

Chris stopped at the edge of the water.

I thought I caught an evil-sounding chuckle from our assailant. Maybe he really was a psycho who was just waiting for us to trespass so he could shoot us and have it be all neat and legal. Or maybe he had just now started thinking about the situation he had gotten himself into. We hadn't been scared off by his rant, and he didn't look like he would have lasted long against Chris. Maybe he was relieved that he had a way out.

"Come on down here and we'll settle this!" We began yelling back at him.

He wasn't moving. His wife had appeared by then and seemed to be trying to diffuse things, though to no avail. His bluff may have been called, but he kept right on screaming.

"I'm gonna call Fish and Wildlife!" he shouted.

"Go ahead!" we both yelled back. "We have all of our licences. Call the police while you're at it!"

"The (#@%*!&!!) access point is three hundred meters upstream, why don't you go (*#%$@!) fish up there?!!"

That was what he was going berserk about?? We were fishing within shouting range of his house?!? I wondered for a moment if he verbally assaulted every fisherman who wandered in too close. He must have really been pissed when 500 guys dressed up as Orcs came through... Still, how could he have been unaware of the access point directly across the river? Sometimes you just find the wrong kind of people living on public access trout streams.

I might have had time for all of those thoughts to run through my mind (except, of course, the bit about the Orcs; that struck me as funny just now), but I didn't have the opportunity to say all of that.

"There is a marked access point right behind us!" I said, pointing over my shoulder to the spot just over the bridge where we had come in.

The shouting match continued for a while longer, but it eventually became clear that we were at a stalemate. In the end he made up some excuse to go back to his house to make a call to someone.

Chris and I made a half-hearted attempt to go back to fishing, but it was no use. We were both too worked up. Maybe there are some leisure activities that still work when you're so agitated you just want to knock someone's teeth out. Kick-boxing, perhaps. Fly fishing, not so much.

I would guess that just about every angler knows the list of things that can go wrong when traveling to fish. Bad weather, delayed flights, lost luggage (God forbid it includes your rods and reels…), or even just a streak of inexplicably poor fishing that happens to coincide with your presence. Chris once had a camera stolen out of his suitcase on the way home from a trip. As if that wasn't bad enough, all the pictures from the best morning of steelhead fishing I've ever had were on that camera. Three bucks, all 15 pounds or better, before noon. I still don't like thinking about that. Some a-hole probably deleted those files to make room for pictures of his cat.

That seems like plenty of potential disasters to worry about, especially when one is contemplating going on that "trip of a lifetime", and possibly spending a little more than they realistically should. Strangely, getting assaulted with rocks by a psycho coke-fiend in a foreign country wasn't on my list before, but I suppose it is now.

We did the only logical thing after a day like that. We headed back to Blenheim, found the first halfway decent looking bar, and proceeded with working our way through the selection of local brews on tap. Funny how that's the logical thing whether your day was great, terrible, or just plain bizarre.

The next day Chris boarded a plane headed home, and I reported for duty at the winery where I would spend the next couple of months making Marlborough Pinot Noir. My bucket-list fishing trip had concluded. So, I didn't cross any exotic (or prehistoric) species off of my list. I had gone to the other side of the world and caught... trout. But hey, I like trout. And who's to say I won't ever do that trip to Scotland for dinosaurs-on-a-dry-fly? It could still happen.

## Fly Fishing the Troutless River

    I'm thankful to the folks at Disney / Pixar. This is about fishing, I promise. Just bear with me. I'm just saying that it's nice that their movies are entertaining for adults as well as kids. They certainly don't have to be to keep the youngins happy. I've sat through a kids movie or two that make performing a self-appendectomy seem like a better way to pass the time. So, as a parent who still has young children (okay, one is still young…), I truly appreciate it. Having said that, I'm now going to take them to task.

    If we're to believe the premise of *Inside Out* (which I dutifully sat through with my daughter), then we are all controlled by the competing interests of five "emotions"; Joy, Fear, Sadness, Disgust, and Anger. Okay, it was a cute movie, but allow me to submit that, at the very least, we should include a "Reason / Judgement" character in the cast, for crying out loud; and, since choosing Lewis Black as the voice of Anger was undoubtedly the best casting decision in the history of cinema, we are going to need someone pretty solid to be the voice of Reason. Leonard Nimoy would be the obvious choice if he were still with us. Hmm… let's go with Wallace Shawn. Stay with me here. Now, if we're talking about a fly fisherman (and we are), we need one more character in there. Let's call him "Fishing Jones". There may be no perfect person to play a character obsessed with fishing, so for now, let's imagine him as Mark Ruffalo.

Rather than being a mess of competing emotions, the captain of this ship is Reason. Ordinarily, Fishing Jones is relatively content to take a back seat to Reason, simply suggesting a fishing trip here and there. However, when denied for too long, Fishing Jones will eventually lose it, turn into The Incredible Hulk, and lay waste to everything in his path. Throw in a clever quip like: "Puny Reason…" as Hulk turns away from the pile of rubble that was once an ordered mind, dons his floppy, fly-adorned fishing hat, grabs his fly rod and strolls off the set, and you have a scene.

I suppose I've experienced this phenomenon a time or two. And let me tell you, Fishing Jones / Hulk doesn't think clearly. He only sees rivers full of rising trout. I guess I could warn you to pay attention to the signs that you might be about to find out for yourself, but why not just tell the story…

I had built a list of rivers that I wanted to get to right away as I was preparing to move to Washington in the summer of 2005. There were some famous names on there, places I might have planned a vacation around just to have the chance to fish them once. Here it was 2009 and I still hadn't made it to the first two on my list. Sure, I'd been fishing, and had been on some good trips, but it still felt like I had just barely scratched the surface of what the Northwest had to offer. It was all right there, just outside my door, waiting for me to come and get it, and yet, time was passing me by.

It was spring in Walla Walla, the time when the wheat fields turn green, and the whole town seems to explode with flowering trees, lining the streets with whites and pinks wherever you look. It always got me thinking about fishing, just like fall. And summer. And winter. Anyway, summer was coming and my wife and I were talking about whether we wanted to attempt our annual camping trip with the family. Our two boys, Ian and James, were ten and nine at the time, and both of them were always up for a camping trip. I was also considering inaugurating them into fly fishing that summer. The wild card was our newest addition to the clan; Josephine, who was only a few months old.

How hard could camping with an infant be? They can't get into that much trouble; about all they do is eat, sleep, and look cute. Okay, they poop and cry quite a bit too, but they also do that at home. When put to a decision as to whether to stay home while the boys and I went camping or come along and have a new baby to care for in camp, my wife chose to come along.

Now the best way to handle this scenario seems obvious enough. Go to the closest place that has a half decent campground and something resembling a fishing spot. Whatever you do, do not choose a location that is far away or unfamiliar. I knew all of that... at least in theory. But what about the boys who are ready for something more interesting than the little campground forty minutes from home with the little stream and little fish? Should they not get their shot at something more adventurous? And what about Dear Old Dad? Back in the Glory Days, sixteen hours of driving in a weekend wasn't unheard of if the fishing was good enough. How the mighty had fallen since then. Dear Old Dad still hadn't been able to pull off the three hour drive to the world famous Deschutes River, even though he'd had four years to git r' done.

Another thing that any serious, experienced fly fisherman knows is to stay away from well-known, ultra-popular destinations on either the Memorial Day or Labor Day weekend. Sadly, even a fisherman who ought to know better can find himself in the same boat as everyone else, with the opportunity to get the whole family group out to one of those primo destinations only coming along on the same three-day weekend that everyone else has, and he can either take it or leave it.

I made a few calls to local businesses around Maupin, the little town that sits right on the river and functions as the unofficial capital of the fishing population that frequents the Deschutes, to inquire about how bad the crowds might be on Memorial Day weekend. I'm not sure what I was expecting to hear. Perhaps it was just an opportunity to rationalize the decision I had pretty much already made. Not surprisingly, mostly what I heard was how Labor Day was the one with the big crowds, and Memorial Day wasn't so bad.

Maybe that little voice in the back of my mind was Reason beginning to recover from the beating he took at the hands of Fishing Jones / Hulk, but it wasn't enough. I had been told by some locals that it would be okay, and that was all I needed to hear.

I told my wife of my plans. She is used to putting up with some borderline obsessive behavior when it comes to fishing, but it usually involves me being missing for a day or two, leaving her to play the role of fishing widow. This time I was planning to drag her along on an adventure that would only make sense to Fishing Jones, an element of personality that she seems to be missing. I think she has a "Cocktail on the Beach in Hawaii Jones". The two can get along if they can compromise on Christmas Island or the Bahamas, but that's another topic entirely.

The plan seemed simple enough: in order to have the best shot at a good camping spot we would have to leave as quickly as possible Friday night after work. That was the way I had always done it back in the day. Get your butt on the road on Friday night and cover as much ground as you can. If we could get going early enough we could set up camp that night and beat the less ambitious souls who waited until Saturday morning to head out.

"Oh by the way, Honey, I did some research and I want to go up around Maupin, so the drive is going to be a bit longer than I originally thought…"

I can't say if she protested. The Hulk's clouded brain couldn't process the response; it was just some muffled sounds like the noises that the adults make in Charlie Brown cartoons. Perhaps she missed the signs and said that she trusted me. Either way the plan remained in place. We had agreed that it would be best for her to drive out Saturday morning with the baby rather than come along on our Friday night drive.

Hulk is generally a pretty grumpy guy, not known for delusional optimism. Why I believed that I could get going quickly on a Friday night with two kids in tow is unclear. Then again, Hulk is also an idiot.

It was 8:00 PM and we hadn't left. The plan wasn't going to work. Reason wouldn't have made such a mistake. Reason doesn't expect that things that have never been will all of a sudden be. Reason wouldn't get up in the morning and stare at the western horizon waiting for the sun to come up, for example, or expect to be able to leave the house with children in a reasonable amount of time. I almost decided to scrap the drive for the night and take the entire troup in the morning, but that would virtually constitute an unconditional surrender. Never! We would try it in spite of very little (okay, zero) chance of success.

It turned out my old Chevy truck wasn't quite able to make the jump to light speed that night. That meant it was around eleven as we were nearing The Dalles. A decision had to be made to either turn and start upriver to the tune of (at least) another hour, or find a motel and spend the night. Back in The Day, when my brother Chris, myself, and our band of intrepid adventurers used to wander far and wide in search of willing trout we wouldn't have hesitated, even if it meant setting up the tent at three in the morning. My band of adventurers on this trip included two half-asleep kids who were not very likely to be of much help with setting up camp in the dark. To be honest, I was pretty tired as well, and wasn't all that excited to keep going. My younger self would have hung his head low to have had to witness the shame of pulling off at a motel rather than pressing on, but so it was.

The master plan had run into its first setback. Anyone who had left from Portland the previous evening would have beaten us to the best camping spots, but seeing as how we were starting two hours closer to the river than they would be, we still had the advantage over those who were planning to head out the next morning. I was determined not to waste that advantage, so we were up early and on the road again.

This where my advanced sales skills came in handy. To save the time that it would have taken to stop for breakfast; I convinced a nine and a ten-year-old boy that a package of powdered doughnuts and some chocolate milk constituted a "good enough" breakfast in a pinch. Yeah, I could sell ice to Eskimos.

It took nearly an hour to get to Maupin, and I couldn't help but think about how we made the right decision by stopping for the night. We still had to go about finding a place to camp. Thinking about the drive that my wife would be doing that morning with a newborn infant in the back seat, I suddenly realized that my life could well be in danger. Of course, we would have to do it again to get home. I put the thought out of my mind; there was a campground to set up and trout to be caught. The plan was to camp and fish the section of river below Maupin. The map showed so many campgrounds and access points that I figured we should be fine, even with some crowds.

The first campgrounds we came to out of town were overflowing with people. Not a good sign, but also not altogether unexpected. As we continued downstream there were indeed many campgrounds, but none had any spaces available. Okay, that's not entirely true. We did find one or two, situated nicely right on the edge of a cliff. Even Hulk could see the problem there.

It wasn't too far before we came to the end of the paved road. There were many miles of dirt road ahead with more campgrounds, and that was no problem in my four-wheel-drive truck. My wife was following in her Toyota Avalon, and this little development couldn't possibly help her mood after the four hour drive. There was nothing else to do but go on. We covered the entire length of the road, checking each campground along the way. Nothing. Every space was full.

The last campground before the end of the road was Mack's Canyon. It was one of the larger sites we had seen, and to my surprise, was only about half full. We were saved, but we had to have gone another hour past Maupin, making for a five hour drive from Walla Walla.

The boys and I set up camp as quickly as possible. We would have to go back to town to meet my wife, who wouldn't have any way of knowing exactly where we were. I could tell the kids were nearing their limit of back seat time, though so far there hadn't been any meltdowns. Still, we needed to get to the fun part pretty quickly or things would begin to spiral towards the abyss. I figured we could have some lunch and get some ice cream in Maupin, and perhaps that would lift everyone's spirits.

There comes a time on some fishing trips when you start thinking about cutting your losses. Maybe you could still get the yard work done, or finish your tax returns on time, or maybe you could do something with your kids that they might enjoy more than spending seven hours in the back seat of a truck. At this point I hadn't so much as wet a line, much less fallen in the river, hooked myself in the face, or taken a wrong turn and spent two hours driving the wrong way in a foreign country. Yet somehow I'd swear I could hear the voice of Reason in the back of my mind; letting me know that I'd fallen for one of the classic blunders, comparable to getting involved in a land war in Asia.

I couldn't give up. It was too late for that. Besides, mine was not a blind mania, leading me like a lemming off the edge of a cliff. There was a purpose; a reason behind my madness. Visions of hungry rainbows rising with reckless abandon to big black stoneflies led me to press on until my goal was accomplished.

That's right, it was supposed to be the perfect time for the stonefly hatch. I would do what needed to be done, then they would understand… Once the boys and I had experienced the epic fishing that only a stonefly hatch can provide, I could always remind my wife of our inadequate life insurance situation before she murdered me.

Now for those of you who have never experienced fly fishing a great trout stream at the peak of a stonefly hatch, let me just tell you, as someone who has spent years fishing some of the most famous rivers of the West from Montana to New Mexico… neither have I. I had only heard stories of how silly the fishing could be. I just missed it once on the Madison in Montana. We were able to raise a few fish who still remembered what a stonefly was, but the hatch had ended, and a few average fish was all we could manage. It didn't seem fair, dammit, and I was going to git 'r done this time.

Once we had camp set up we walked down to the river to take a look. The bushes and tall grass along the river were infested with stoneflies. Victory was within my grasp, I just needed to punch it across the goal line…

For those not familiar with the Northwest, it's actually not all rain and evergreens. Once you get east of the Cascades, the climate changes drastically. Eastern Oregon and Washington are dry regions. The low lying areas are home to various types of agriculture and the landscape contains expansive areas of flat, relatively featureless land. Where you find mountains they remind one more of the terrain of the Rocky Mountains than that of the lush, green, often wet landscape one finds in the coastal areas of the Northwest. Huge rivers run through this part of the world, and trees or no, they form some spectacular canyons. The Snake joins the Columbia in eastern Washington, forming one of the largest rivers in the world, draining an area approximately the size of France. The many tributaries of this great river system are enough to provide a lifetime of fishing opportunities.

Though it is not very far to the east of the Cascades, the Deschutes is definitely a dry-side river. Most of the lower river (below Maupin) is surrounded by high canyon walls, often rising hundreds of feet above the river itself. Though not necessarily what one would expect from a Northwestern steelhead and trout stream, the beauty of the place is easy to appreciate. Summer weather is hot, and it is a popular destination for Portlanders (particularly around Memorial Day, as I was quickly finding out) who are looking for some fun in the sun after the long, rainy winter and mostly rainy spring.

It was mid-day when we met up with my wife in Maupin. We had a little picnic in a small park in town and found a place to get everyone some ice cream. The kids were grumpy, but I assured everyone that the worst was over and the fun was about to start. It took another hour to make the drive back to the campground, making it mid-afternoon before we were all in camp and ready to begin our trip. I rigged the rods up and slipped into my waders as quickly as I could and the boys and I headed down to fish the stretch of river right below our camp.

It looked like decent water, and my hopes were high. There were still plenty of stoneflies in the grass and bushes, but I didn't see any on the water, and no trout were rising. No problem. I rigged everyone up with some variation of a stonefly nymph and we started working the water.

Now the kids, of course, are not the most patient anglers. I knew there would have to be some action relatively quickly to keep them interested. Strangely, nothing wanted our stonefly imitations. It must have been close to an hour before a fish took my nymph.

"Here we go guys!" I yelled to the boys, who I had fishing as close to me as possible.

"Watch what I do!"

Neither of them had dealt with big trout on fly rods before, though they had both practiced quite a bit in the front yard. I was talking through the process of gaining control of a running trout in current when I caught sight of the fish: a sucker. My spirits dropped. Why were the trout not cooperating? Stoneflies are supposed to be like catnip to these things.

Around then the wind started picking up and the boys lost interest and headed back to camp. I, of course, could not give up. This could not be right. The bugs were around (though not, it would seem, on the water). All I had to do was stick with it and the fishing would turn on.

Another hour passed, and the only thing that turned on was gale-force winds. Eventually I had to head back to camp in inglorious defeat, knowing that the camping that night would be unpleasant if not outright impossible if the wind didn't die down.

Back in camp everyone was upset. The wind was blowing so hard that it was freaking out the baby, who had been screaming. Apparently the kids had come back down to the river to find me and couldn't, and were afraid that I might have been swept away and drowned.

It was late afternoon. Our camp was all set up. It was too late and we were too tired to try to pack up and move. We would just have to ride it out. We managed to get through dinner with the wind howling through the camp. It wasn't letting up. I couldn't help remembering an ill-fated night I spent in a tent with some friends years earlier when we were forced to hold up the sides of the tent until dawn as the blasting wind was trying to flatten it on top of us. No sleep was had that night. But even that night had a silver lining: no infant in the tent. We retreated to the "safety" of the tent early and hoped for the best. The wind finally died down around 11:00 PM. I guess it could have been worse.

We awoke the next morning to clear skies and no wind. The campground was a bit messy from having endured the relentless wind during the night, but we cleaned it back up and proceeded with our usual camp breakfast of pancakes and bacon. I put a plan together to explore the river that day in search of spots that might offer better holding water for trout. I was nowhere near ready to concede defeat.

With the group I had we wouldn't be fishing hard all day by any means, and I wanted my wife to get a chance to get out on the water as well, which meant I would be taking a turn with the baby on dry land. We hit a couple of good looking spots on the river, with my wife and I taking turns fishing (by taking turns I mean that she did actually get to fish, but not exactly half of the time) and watching Josephine, who didn't do much besides just lay there and look cute.

Ian and James were goofing off around the water, and were reasonably content to do so. Apparently they had decided that there weren't any fish in the river, and so trying to catch something that wasn't there didn't hold much appeal. For the moment it was fine, as it was better that they were playing happily than not, but it did cause me some concern for their futures as fly fishermen in the Northwest. After all, if you're going to stop fishing any time that the evidence suggests that your quarry doesn't really exist, then you'll never make much of a steelheader.

It would be up to me to get into some, and then maybe they would get interested again. I had all of their stuff ready to go for when the trout started biting. I threw every variation of a stonefly pattern, both dry and wet, at any piece of water that looked like it might hold a trout. I even tried an assortment of standard nymphs and dries that generally work on most any river in the West. Once again, nothing was interested. The only difference from the previous day was that I did see one rainbow come up and take something off the top. Since I also had just about decided that the river was actually devoid of any aquatic life forms, it was reassuring in a way to see that there were, in fact, trout in the river. Then again, considering the heat and my mental condition at the time, I had to admit the possibility that it was a mirage.

By early afternoon I had realized and accepted my fate. I found one more stretch of river that looked safe and easy to wade and set Doreen (my very patient and understanding wife) up to spend a little time fishing. She began working the water while I kept the little one entertained. She seemed determined to give it her best shot, and was working hard to make casts into some difficult spots. Bless her little heart, she thought there were fish in the river.

I could still hope for one pleasant night in camp, but we would need to find a less exposed campsite. As luck would have it, some of them had already cleared out a bit, even though it was still just the middle of the long weekend. We decided to leave our camp intact, but to take everything we needed to make dinner and enjoy some time around a fire and go find someplace that looked like it would be well sheltered.

The camp fire is the kids' favorite part of camping, so at least we had one good night to remember. We had no way of knowing for sure if our original camp site was getting clobbered with wind, but we decided to spend the evening in our new location just to be safe. We would head back to the tent just before bed time so as to avoid having to sit there in the wind for any longer than necessary.

Any thoughts of having our luck finally change on this trip disappeared when we rolled back into our camp site late that evening. The wind was blowing hard, and our tent, though it had been staked down and loaded with our gear, had blown away. It was sitting on its' side pressed against the wall of bushes that lined the river. Were it not for the bushy barrier, our tent with all of our stuff in it may would have ended up floating downstream to eventually be chewed up in the turbines at The Dalles Dam.

We couldn't leave it that way, no matter how tempting it was to say the heck with it and go get a motel room. We had to rebuild the camp, with the wind still ripping through our site. Besides, it was already late, around 10:00 PM. To head back to town and get a motel room would take an hour of driving, plus however long it took to clean up the camp. Of course I had gone out and purchased a nice big new tent to accommodate our larger group. It offered the convenience of being tall enough for a grown man to stand up inside it, a luxury I was not used to in a tent. This also made it something like a gigantic sail in the wind.

If only I'd had the foresight to set up the video camera on a tripod to film our attempts to get the ($#@!!*&!) thing back up; we'd have picked up ten grand on *America's Funniest Home Videos* for sure; not to mention the certainty of being able to sell the rights to the story to the folks at *National Lampoon*.

Oh well, I suppose the camera probably would have blown over and exploded had I thought of it. Besides, Chevy Chase is too old now to play me in the *Fishing Vacation* movie. Anyway, we finally managed to get the tent back up and get ourselves stowed away in it just in time for the wind to stop, again right around 11:00 PM.

There was nothing left that could go wrong. All we had to do was get up the next morning, feed everyone, break camp, and head for home. Of course, there was the five hour drive with an infant in the back seat to worry about, but how bad could that be after what we had just been through?

The next morning the desert sun wasted no time in heating things up as we broke camp and loaded up the truck. I had already worked up a good sweat when I happened to look over at my wife's car and noticed the flat tire.

I suppose I should have seen that coming. What more fitting end could there be to such a trip than to turn myself into a (dirt) sugar-cookie just before starting a long drive? Of course, there's just one catch to changing a tire on that Avalon. You need a hex wrench to remove the "hub cap" to get to the lug nuts. Having been in this situation before, I had stashed one in the glove box.

I've always had certain psychic abilities when it comes to seeing all the little things that can and will go wrong in any given endeavor; even to the point that it puzzles me when everyone around me can't see them as well. It feels like a curse for the most part, as it only leads to a reputation for being negative. Strangely, no one ever seems to remember the warnings when it hits the fan just like you predicted. In any case, this whole trip was an obvious trap that I normally wouldn't have fallen for, but like I said, Hulk doesn't think clearly.

That time had passed, and clarity had returned to me. At that moment I realized that what I had was not some random, mildly annoying psychic ability. I was, in fact, The Chosen One. Chosen by the universe to receive the Full Revelation of Murphy's Law. Through trial by fire, I had been given complete comprehension of the one true law that governs the universe: Anything That Can Go Wrong Will Go Wrong, And At The Worst

Possible Time. The details of exactly when and how things would go wrong were like a whirlwind in my head, but I could see them all, though surely such knowledge could never have been intended for the minds of mere mortals.

Or, to put it more succinctly, I knew the (%$##@!!*?$) hex wrench wasn't going to be in the glove box.

Yes, I looked in the glove box (for the benefit of any newlyweds who might be reading this; should you ever find yourself in such a situation, telling your wife that you didn't look because you have decided that you have quasi-god-like powers and therefore don't need to will not improve the situation in any way). No, it wasn't there. Doreen had removed it the last time she cleaned out her car.

The realization that a silver lining had just fallen in my lap didn't hit me right away, though it was just in time to halt an oncoming cerebral aneurism. My wife was now guilty of a stupid mistake as well (that actually makes two if you count trusting me) and wouldn't be able to give me nearly as much of a hard time over this fiasco as she otherwise would have.

Be that as it may, we were still stuck. I could spend an hour (each way) driving to Maupin to look for a set of hex wrenches… on a federal holiday, in a town that has a population of 423, and a total geographical area of less than a square mile-and-a-half. If all else failed, I could call a tow truck. I would need to drive back into cell phone range first, of course, and they might even get to us before nightfall. By comparison, climbing to the top of the nearest cliff and hurling myself off would take maybe twenty minutes.

As I was surveying the surrounding canyon for the ideal spot to jump, I realized that there was one other possibility. The last person left in the campground (besides ourselves) was hitching up his trailer to leave. As much as I may be loath to ask for help (or directions) until there truly is no other choice, I had to admit that it was (marginally) preferable to leaping two hundred feet into an open grave.

He had a complete set of hex wrenches (which could only encourage my wife to insist on more of this strange "asking for help" behavior in the future). At least it offered an opportunity to find out what kind of luck he'd had fishing. He said they had floated the river all the previous day and only caught a couple of fish. At least it wasn't just me.

The drive home went about the way you might expect. Of course, if you're like me, you would expect that little Josephine was going to cry the entire way, and that another tire on the Avalon was going to slowly go flat. The five hour drive ended up taking more like eight, but all the stops to try to comfort the baby gave us a chance to put air in that tire, allowing us to kill the proverbial two birds with one stone. Always look on the bright side of life.

Thankfully for little Josephine, she won't remember any of it. Unfortunately for me, everyone else will remember our trip to the Big Troutless.

Lest there be any confusion, I should explain that the Troutless isn't a real river per se; or at least not in the stationary, three-dimensional, linear time and space sense of the word. It isn't a Karmic punishment either, brought down upon those who would drag their family along on an ill-conceived adventure to satisfy their own lust for fish. You certainly can't avoid it by skipping the Deschutes, which remains one of the West's great trout and steelhead rivers.

The Troutless is more like a randomly occurring special-temporal anomaly, and even if you keep Reason and Fishing Jones living in perfect harmony at all times, you may still find yourself wandering its' banks someday, plying its' infinitely empty waters in perpetual befuddlement. As for the other disasters you may encounter when Fishing Jones takes over, well, that's all on you, so do yourself a favor; go fishing, before it's too late.

# Cosmic Justice
## And Other Perils of Raising Fly Fishermen

I watched with satisfaction as the fly line unfurled perfectly. The leader straightened just above the water, and my tiny dry fly settled gently in the path of a big rainbow that was feeding sporadically against the far bank.

"That might do it…" I thought to myself.

# Cosmic Justice

The fish moved to investigate the fly, drifting briefly with the current as it tried to decide. It seemed a bit too long, like a refusal was imminent, but at the last moment it snatched the fly from the surface and turned back toward its lie. As I set the hook my 4-weight bent double and began pulsing with the weight of the fish. Before long I was holding another perfect specimen in the icy current of the South Platte River, admiring it briefly before it swam away. Pausing to take it all in; the stream, the steep canyon walls adorned with evergreens, the crisp, cold air of early spring in the Rockies, I couldn't help hoping that it would always be this way.

So went much of my twenties; wandering the trout streams of the Rocky Mountains with a fly rod in hand. I never planned on slowing down. Not that I planned on being a *real* "trout bum" per se. I had a job, and I wanted a family; but I figured I would just bring them along. My kids would be roll casting before they could walk.

Since then I've learned a few things. For example: human children, contrary to popular belief, do have instincts. In their first few years of life, they instinctively try to harm or kill themselves given any opportunity to do so. Left to their own devices, their chances of survival are approximately equal to those of a kamikaze pilot. Take them outdoors and they'll quickly identify any cliff, dead drop, or bottomless pit in any given area by sprinting at top speed directly towards it. Dangerous objects left within their reach will not only be handled, but potentially consumed. A hand-tied Royal Wulff might as well be an M&M. As they get older, this tendency (slowly) fades away, replaced by a desire to harm their siblings instead. And so, anything that facilitates the injury process begins to seem ill advised, including flinging a hook through the air past their own (or each other's) faces.

So, I decided that learning to fly cast could wait a little while, and both of our boys learned to fish the old-fashioned way; with a Spongebob spin-caster and Power Bait at the local lake. We would work our way up to fly fishing; and before you knew it, the three of us would be standing side by side in a pristine mountain stream, casting dry flies to rising trout.

To complicate matters, I'd traded in the Rocky Mountains for the rolling hills, wheat fields, and vineyards of eastern Washington; and now found myself in unfamiliar surroundings. Trout streams weren't so plentiful as they were in Colorado, but they could be found. There was a little tributary with a little campground not far from home that was perfect for their first overnight fishing trip. In the fall it would host a run of steelhead, but the mid-summer flows were so low that one could only manage to drown in it by falling in face-first and refusing to roll onto one's side. By then the boys were reasonably sure-footed and no longer seemed determined to end their own lives prematurely, so I figured we were good to go. The fish were sized to match the stream, but it hardly mattered. The boys got 'em, using flies fished with casting bubbles and the old spin-casters.

Perhaps it was just a trickle, but it probably hadn't seemed that way to the boys, who were six and eight at the time. They'd waded fearlessly. They'd defeated the mighty (4-inch juvenile) Oncorhynchus mykiss. It was encouraging. By the next summer I had begun thinking seriously about teaching them to fly fish. I occasionally took out a rod and tried to show them how to cast, without garnering a whole lot of interest. What we needed was a *real* trout fishing trip.

The Wallowa River in the Blue Mountains of eastern Oregon was just what the doctor ordered. It even reminded me of my beloved Rocky Mountain trout streams, complete with evergreen forests growing in an otherwise dry landscape. We waded some of the easier runs, and fished once again with casting bubbles and flies. Everything was going according to plan. Trout were caught, pictures were taken, everyone was happy. Ian (the older boy) was completely gung-ho about fishing. He couldn't be dragged away from the water. Victory!!

Oh, but what would life be without little twists of fate? Things were going so well that when Ian begged me to let him try the fly rod I agreed, despite his lack of training. Within seconds the hook had found purchase in flesh, and just like that, defeat was snatched from the jaws of victory. I can still hear the sound of his nine-year-old voice yelling: "I never want to go fishing again!"

I didn't bring up fly fishing again until spring of 2009. James was nine and Ian was about to turn eleven. I was determined to make their first "real" fly fishing trip memorable, like mine had been so many years earlier. It was an adventure that changed my entire perspective, and left me with memories for a lifetime. Was it too much to hope for that I could create such an experience for the boys?

For such a thing, nothing less than a world-class trout stream would do. After finally completing some basic casting instruction, I picked a famous river (one that I had never fished) and hit the road with the family.

Fishing seems like such a simple thing; an enjoyable pastime handed down smoothly from fathers to sons from time immemorial. The road to our first fly fishing trip hadn't exactly been simple, but surely a father attempting to pass along such a worthwhile tradition to his children would be worthy of some sort of Karmic reward. But then, it's never seemed to me that Karma (or any sort of cosmic justice, poetic or otherwise) has anything to do with fishing. If it does, then I must have been Vlad the Impaler in a previous life. No, the rules that govern the fishing universe look suspiciously like Murphy's Law to me, and that trip proved it once and for all. We drove way too far, our tent blew away in a wind storm, and we caught nothing. Strike two.

Things were getting desperate. My suggestions that fly fishing really was fun were beginning to draw the kind of looks usually reserved for eating broccoli or trips to the dentist. I could feel my window of opportunity closing.

Time to pull out all the stops. I needed nothing less than a world-class trout stream, and I had just one ace left to play. It was a bit far, but the fishing would be worth it. I'd been hesitant to take the kids there sooner. Most of the good runs involved tricky wading and lots of casting obstructions. There was also some poison ivy and the occasional snake.

Taking them there when they were really little wouldn't have made much sense; after all they'd always found ways to put themselves in harm's way right at home, there was no need to travel for that. But now they were ready.

Ian was just about to turn twelve. James had recently turned ten. James was still showing some interest in fly fishing, but Ian appeared to have gotten over it entirely. He wanted to go camping with us, but let it be known that he didn't plan to fish much. He was bringing a couple of books to read in camp instead. It's not like I was unhappy that he was an avid reader, but I still hoped that there was a brown trout out there that could change his mind.

We arrived at the campground around mid-day on a Saturday. There weren't too many other people around, and the adjacent run was empty of fishermen. That was particularly helpful; the Campground Pool is the easiest part of the river to fish. It's a perfect little spot. Sixty feet across, with a gentle slope down to a depth of perhaps four feet in the middle, with a slightly riffled, walking-speed current. Just a couple of trees on the close side leaves plenty of room for casting. The opposite side of the river is lined with brush and set against a ridge of towering rock formations that keeps sunlight off the water until mid-morning.

It was too early in the year for really hot weather, but the sun was high overhead and the sky a cloudless blue. That would be the kiss of death at some rivers, but not this place. There wasn't any activity to be seen, but I knew the fish were there. They could be taken on nymphs until mid-afternoon, when the real hatches would start.

We set up with the three of us fishing side-by-side. It seemed like another lifetime when I'd stood in a Rocky Mountain trout stream imagining this moment so many years before. We started casting. Behind the soft *whoosh* of fly lines cutting through the air, I swear I could hear the soundtrack from *A River Runs Through It* playing in the background.

A trout took my fly. I talked through what I was doing as I played the fish, a pretty nineteen inch brown, into the net. As I released it I looked up and said to the lads:

"Your turn, boys. There are plenty of these in here."

Anticipation was high as the fish became more active. They were feeding just below the surface now, shifting left and right to grab the emergers, their sleek forms clearly visible despite the slightly off-color water. They were big. Any minute now...

"I'm cursed." I heard Ian say as he walked behind me.

The soundtrack in my mind screeched to a halt with the sound of a needle scraping across a record.

He held up his rod as he walked by. It was decorated with the kind of compound tangle that can only be achieved by continuing to cast after you've already put a really horrendous knot in your leader.

"You're not cursed, you just need to give it a little more effort." I replied as I snapped back to reality.

What could I do? He was headed back to camp to read a book, and you're not allowed to scold a kid for reading. That's on page one of the Parent's Handbook. Rule 1: Never discipline a toddler using a mace, flail, or morning-star. Rule 2: No scolding of children for reading.

I let it go for the moment, figuring I could coach one boy at a time more effectively anyway. We didn't have to wait long. A big trout took James' fly and proceeded to bolt this way and that around the pool, slipping free in the process.

"Remember to keep pressure on them. They'll spit a barbless hook easily if you let your line go slack. Don't worry, you'll get another chance."

Fish number two stayed on the line a bit longer, but snapped the tippet when James tucked the butt of the rod into his stomach and the reel handle caught against his vest.

James' shoulders dropped a bit as he stared at his flyless leader. He almost had that one.

"Reminds me of my first attempts at managing a big trout on a fly rod." I offered. "I got cleaned out a few times before I figured out what to do with my hands. Just remember to keep your reel clear of your body. If they go to run and the reel can't spin freely, your line will break, just like it did there."

Fish number three. It took off downstream. James let him run, then gained line back slowly. Looking good. I kept the coaching to a minimum; he was doing it all right.

Another run, shorter than the first, but still strong. Again, James responded properly, feeling what the fish was doing, waiting for his chance to gain ground. Before long, he had it in close and I got a good look at it.

"That's a good fish James." I said, trying to contain my excitement. "Just keep the tension on him, he's almost in."

I don't know which of us was more excited when we netted him. He was a gorgeous twenty inch brown.

"That's a really nice one." I said as we admired the fish in the net.

His back was virtually solid spots, with copper flanks and a butter-yellow belly. He was more than I had hoped for. A quick measure confirmed my estimate.

"A twenty-incher. Well done, James." I added, holding out my hand for a congratulatory shake.

We snapped a quick hero shot, then watched as the fish disappeared back into the depths of the pool.

It was a perfect moment. Well almost, anyway. Something was missing...

The fish continued biting, and before long I had a good one of my own on the line. Another group of fishermen had come along by then and they wandered over to watch me land it.

"Nice fish" One of the men said.

"Yeah, there are some good ones in here." I replied as I released the trout, and then casually added: "*My ten-year-old just caught a twenty-incher on his own...*"

The whole group seemed visibly tickled by this, and I could only imagine that they were all fathers themselves.

"All-right" one of them said.

"Way to go Dad." offered another.

My first opportunity to brag. Now it was perfect.

The boys' favorite part of camping is the campfire, and they were anxious to get to it, so we didn't stay out late. And, like every male under thirty, Ian and James react to a campfire by turning into certified pyromaniacs. As they happily incinerated everything that wasn't necessary for our survival, a thought took shape in the back of my mind...

The next morning we put in an hour of fishing without any action, and that was enough for the boys. James had been away from video games for over twenty-four hours and would start showing signs of withdrawals before much longer. Ian was bored and wanted to goof off with James. They were done, but that same thought still haunted me...

There was a hog out there. There had to be. The fish were in the best shape that I'd seen. Spots that held seventeen inch fish in previous years held fat nineteens and twenties this year. Spots that had held twenties before, well, who knows what might be there now? I had to find out.

I pulled over at one of my favorite runs on the drive out. Ian and James were content to watch movies in the truck for a while, but still, I told myself I would only fish for five or ten minutes and then pack it in if nothing took.

The run was a virtual rock garden, above the surface and below. Sixty yards long, five feet deep in the middle, with moderate current and prime lies everywhere. Below the run was a broad, slow, deep pool. The close bank was steep and rocky, a good place to twist an ankle. The far bank was lined with bushes, and the close side only had breaks in the brush for the big piles of rocks.

I scrambled down to the water at the back end of the run to begin fishing my way up. I placed a cast just upstream of one of the larger sunken rocks and let it drift past, then down through the deep trough below, and there it was. When I set the hook it turned downstream and took off like a rocket.

I couldn't turn it, even in the slower pool below the run. If there had been any shore at all I would have been running to try to keep up, but the bank was completely socked in with heavy brush, and all I could do was slowly make my way through stomach-high water that obscured the shin-cracking boulders below.

The fish was into my backing quickly and I couldn't seem to do anything about it. I followed as far as I could, but it wasn't just heading downstream, it was making a run for the far side. The pool was one of the widest, deepest, and slowest parts of the river. It must have been a hundred feet across to the other side, because all of my fly line was out. There was no way to follow.

I was going to have to make a stand, hoping the hook wouldn't pull free as the weight of the current pushed against ninety feet of fly line. It was a painstaking affair, slowly gaining back line little by little. When I finally got it in close enough to see me it turned and muscled back out again, its head pointing down, still strong enough to strip out line. I knew it was a big brown trout by then, but it felt a little like trying to land a Chinook on 5X tippet and a size fourteen hook.

While the fish was focused on maintaining a safe distance from me, I slowly managed to work my way back upstream. When I got close enough again I started calling for Ian, and eventually he heard me and came down to the river to see what all the fuss was about.

"What's going on?" Ian called out from shore.

"A huge fish!" I yelled back from downstream.

Several times I worked it in almost within net range, I just couldn't turn its head. The final tug-of-war seemed to go on and on, but I finally brought the beast to the net, and by that I mean that about two-thirds of him would fit in the net.

"Do you have a tape measure?" Ian asked.

"I do." I answered, pulling my little retractable tape measure from my vest.

Holding him just underwater with his head in the net, we laid him as flat as we could.

"Twenty-four inches!" Ian said.

"Twenty-three actually.'" I replied, making sure I got an accurate measurement. "But look at the girth on this thing!"

He was a fantastic specimen of a wild brown trout. Even the big, healthy fish we had caught the day before would have looked like eels next to him. This one was more like a football with fins. With an almost greenish-yellow color overall, he could literally vanish against the stream bottom, even in plain sight. He had the thick, powerful shoulders of a mature buck, but he didn't look like a gnarly old fish. He struck me as a young, healthy fish, which means he may still be out there, and he could be the size of a small dolphin by now. Maybe I had some good Karma going for me after all.

Raising fly fishermen turned out to be quite a bit more challenging than I imagined way back in the day. Whether it was fate, or Karma, or Murphy's Law that kept getting in the way I couldn't say; but that three-man trip to fly fish a great trout stream almost never happened. It seemed like such a simple thing. Perhaps in my next life, so long as I'm not a blood-drinking tyrannical eastern European despot, I think I'll stay closer to great trout streams and see if that helps.

Okay, it's also possible that my schemes to make their first fly fishing trip as memorable as mine may have served to overcomplicate things just a bit. So, when I thought she was ready, I went ahead and took their little sister to a trout farm to try out her new fly rod. She was six. Maybe it wasn't the family Maclean casting to wild trout in the sparkling riffles of the Blackfoot River; she still thought it was the best day ever, so I'm counting that as a win.

Ian and James are teenagers now, and their lives are busy with school, work, friends, and girls. I find myself wishing once again for something that isn't terribly realistic; that life would become less complicated; that it would be simple the way it was when they were little, when everyone's schedule wasn't so crazy. The three of us could just go fishing. But life generally doesn't work that way. They'll just get busier. They'll go off to college, get jobs, and get married. Then, one day, there'll be grandchildren… They'll be roll-casting before they can walk.

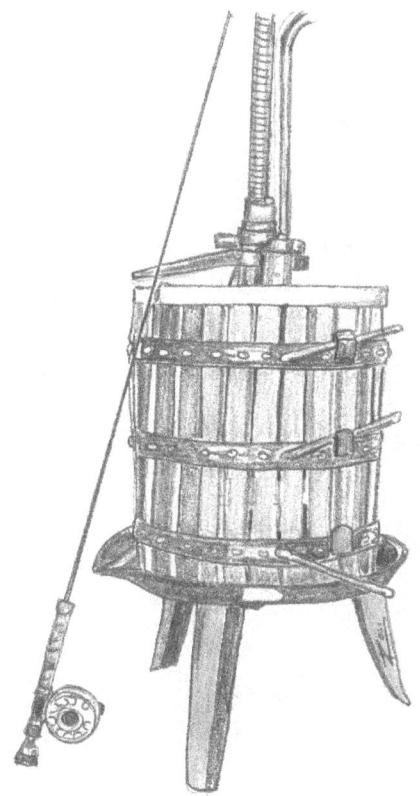

## "Winter" Steelheading

You couldn't ask for a better hobby than fly fishing. A trip to the river can restore the soul, recharge the batteries, and wash away worldly concerns. Take your pick of clichés, fly fishing has got it covered.

Things can get a little dicey when it becomes more than a hobby. You'll certainly hear a number of opinions on the relative merits and downfalls of the life of a fly fishing fanatic. These people are passionate to the point of obsession, so you'll rarely hear them disparage the sport they love. Still, if you think you are in danger of becoming one of these wayward souls, it would be unwise to ignore the guy who tells you that fly fishing ruins lives, and recounts the loss of jobs, wives or girlfriends, and even certain material possessions considered all but vital to one's existence as a result of an obsession with fly fishing.

You can call these guys trout bums (or steelhead bums here in the Northwest), but they don't exactly fit the traditional definition of a bum. Aren't bums supposed to be lazy and unmotivated? Try applying that definition to someone who goes out in the dead of winter in the Pacific Northwest to spend the day standing in the river, making the same spey cast over and over again in the cold and rain, hoping for the unlikely tug of a steelhead on the end of his line. A whole host of descriptive adjectives come to mind, but "unmotivated" is not among them.

But what about those of us who have spent our lives teetering between the life of a normal, responsible adult and that of a fanatic, not willing to fully give up on either? The balancing act can get pretty interesting. One way of keeping the scales balanced is to work at something that inspires you in similar ways to your fishing obsession. Maybe that's the only way to prevent us from dropping off of the grid entirely; disappearing into the woods and emerging again only occasionally with a scraggly beard, smelling of fish, and looking only to replenish our supply of beer and tippet spools before we vanish once again. Okay, so I'm exaggerating a bit, but you get the idea.

My balancing act has been between fishing and wine. I picked up the wine bug while working in dining rooms as an undergraduate at the University of Arizona, and after selling it for a number of years, I got the chance to make wine for a living when I ended up in Walla Walla. That move also precipitated a change in the focus of my fly fishing from trout to steelhead, and that made for one heck of a conflict of interest.

The wine grape harvest, which, of course, happens in the fall, consumes every waking moment of a winemaker's time for a couple of months or more; nights, weekends, everything. Of course this coincides with the absolute best time to target steelhead on the fly on the greatest rivers of the inland Northwest, particularly the Grande Ronde and the Clearwater. The smaller, lesser known tributaries that I liked to fish closer to home were about the same.

If one chose to go west toward the Deschutes or Klickitat, the drive was longer and the fish would be in earlier, but fall was still the best time. I always went somewhere just before harvest started, but whether I was successful or not, I knew that the fishing would be at its' best when I had no way of going.

I loved making wine, and giving up a career that I loved just to go fishing didn't seem like a rational decision, at least to the half of my personality that still qualified as a normal, responsible adult. Still, at some level I would spend the fall months thinking about all of the steelhead swimming past unmolested (at least by me). Of course, every fisherman I knew in Walla Walla would make sure to help me out with reports of all the epic fishing that I was missing.

"I got fourteen hook-ups this morning! Are you gonna get a day off anytime soon?"

"No. Thanks for sharing, though…"

We would stay busy for the rest of the year at the winery, though the really insane schedule would generally be over by Thanksgiving. There would be newly barreled wines to attend to, the secondary fermentation (also known as the malo-lactic fermentation) to manage, and older vintages still in barrels that would need some attention as well. With Holiday events at the winery and Christmas to prepare for at home, I could stay too busy to fish for the rest of the year. To get in a day of fall steelheading, I had to find a way to sneak my exhausted behind out the instant things slowed down near the end of harvest for a single day on a local stream. If I couldn't manage to find a day then, it could be the next year before I got out again.

In 2010 we had a late harvest. That meant a little more time in the late summer to squeeze in some steeelheading. I had one successful outing to the Klickitat, which I had been meaning to fish since I first decided to move to Washington, and a couple of other days out that resulted in a broken rod tip but no fish. That late start meant a late finish, and the Holidays were upon us by the time I came up for air on the other side of harvest. There was no time to squeeze in a day on the Tucannon in November.

A trip that becomes an annual ritual, even a little single day affair like my fall trip to the Tucannon, can become an angler's way of marking the passing of the years, making it far more valuable than the single fish or two it might produce would warrant. I had managed to find a way to squeeze it in for the past several years, and in the course of doing so, had learned the river well enough that I could virtually count on getting a fish if I could just get there; but there was nothing I could do about it. I would have to wait. The fall weather turned to winter as I went to work and came home again one day after another.

Losing a trip that's on your fishing calendar from day one every year can stick in your craw with surprising tenacity. 2010 would be the first year I hadn't managed to get to the Tucannon for steelhead since I had first discovered the place, and my 2009 trip had only produced a single hook-up with a four pound fish... that spit the hook in about twelve seconds. I'd even begun to get that "home water" feeling about the place by then, so putting up a bagel two years in a row wasn't going to work.

The year was drawing to a close, and my time was running out, at least if I wanted to get my Tucannon steelhead for 2010. To make things even more interesting, we were having quite the little cold snap as December drew to a close. New Year's Eve was on the weekend that year; my last chance to get to my home river before 2011.

Perhaps you might still think that so much concern over getting a steelhead before the end of a particular year might seem (just a tad) obsessive. Hang on, you don't know everything just yet. 2010 was the year of my fortieth birthday; it was in July to be specific. I figured if a guy can't add a top of the line fly rod to his collection on such an important birthday, and one that could be looked at as an occasion that requires some consolation for the "official" end of one's youth to boot, then, well, when could you?

I hadn't picked up a real top-of-the-line fly rod in quite a few years, and I was looking for the perfect rod for fishing summer steelhead in small streams. A ten foot seven-weight seemed like the ticket, and I spared no expense. It cast like a dream, punching line into the wind in ways my old six-weight never could, or at least it did at the park near my house. I was dying to get my new baby out on the water. Well, half a year later, I had caught exactly zero fish with my new baby. You may not agree, but I figured that going fishing come hell or high water seemed like the only rational choice.

It was frosty that morning as I climbed into the truck to head off to the river. The truck had been warming up for a bit when I got under way, so I didn't spend much time exposed to the cold. When you're well protected in a warm vehicle, the only thing you really notice on such a morning is that the scenery is quite spectacular. The Blue Mountains, which create the scenic background to the east of Walla Walla, were blanketed in snow from top to bottom. Fields of frosted wheat stubble shimmering in the early morning sun covered the rolling hills along the highway as I made my way past Waitsburg and Dayton.

This part of the state, with its' seemingly endless fields of grain crops, scattered patches of brush, and small, tree-lined streams always gets me thinking about pheasants. Another favorite target that has a fall season. What can you do?

As I passed the bank in Dayton I just caught the temperature reading on the electronic banner display out of the corner of my eye. Did it say four degrees Fahrenheit? Holy frostbite, Batman. It hadn't been that cold in Walla Walla, had it? Oh well, I was committed to going one way or another.

There was a thick layer of fog hanging directly over the river as it came into view. You don't see a lot of fog back in Walla Walla, so this was a strange and unexpected sight. As I drove down into it I couldn't help thinking how the scene looked like an old movie set; with the fog and leafless trees, all that was missing was the Hound of the Baskervilles. I could almost hear Basil Rathbone's voice in the back of my mind warning me to stay off the moors. No problem, Basil. I'll be in the river if you (or the Hound) need me.

The lower Tucannon River runs through rolling hills that are home primarily to ranches. It flows through the tiny town of Starbuck on its' way to empty into the Snake River just a few miles from town. This is the kind of place, along with a few areas in Idaho that I have visited, that would be a pretty good spot to hold up for the collapse of civilization, especially if you had a zombie apocalypse to contend with. There are very few people (potential zombies) around, there is a fresh water source, game and fish (in addition to steelhead, there are some trout, a small salmon run, and I had seen deer and pheasants around the stream as well). If you were to exhaust the supply of wild game, there are still the cows from the surrounding ranches to keep you in hamburgers for as long as you like. Of course, that would be assuming that the ranch owners had become zombies and changed their preference from double cheeseburgers to brains.

When I climbed out of the truck my illusion was shattered. The sparkling winter scene that I had been enjoying on the drive from the safety of my warm, cozy truck was in fact a clever ruse meant to lure me to a certain and horrible death from hypothermia. The frigid air bit into my face and hands, and for the first time I started thinking about calling this whole crazy idea off. It hadn't been this cold back in Walla Walla…

I stopped doubting the four degrees thing; I even wondered if it might be colder than that, as the sun wasn't getting through to the river at all. The few minutes it took to rig up my rod and tie on a fly was all my bare hands could take, and some hand warming in the still-running truck was needed before I could go on.

Steam was rising off the surface of the little stream, which was maybe twenty feet across at this point. Snow covered most of the rocky shoreline, and something about the way the light was filtering through the fog made the water appear to be a deep cobalt blue. A bridge marked the boundary of the fishable part of the river, and I planned to start there and work my way up to the best lie in the area, a nice little trough perhaps seventy feet up.

As I worked my way down to the water, I couldn't help thinking about how bad it would be to fall in. It wasn't like I never slipped in a river.

Still time to change my mind; go get a cup of coffee somewhere, tell everyone I went out and didn't get anything. No, I can do this. There's a fish in there, and I can put a fly in front of him.

Time was a factor. My hands, even with gloves on, wouldn't last long before I would need to get back to the truck to warm them up. Everything that got wet and then touched air was freezing instantly; I could get off maybe two casts before having to knock the ice out of my guides again. My waders were freezing at the point where they touched the water.

No time to be thorough, I put a cast or two through each of the best holding spots, including the cut bank on the near side. The trough was going to be the spot, and I wanted to get to it before my first warm-up break.

The fish was at the bottom of the trough, which was impressively deep considering the size of the stream. He made a half-hearted attempt to go for a run downstream, but I was able to turn him before he got too far. The fight was a rather short affair, not surprising in the super cold conditions. I landed him quickly and saw that he was a hatchery fish; a colorful buck of about four pounds, with a bright green back, and pink stripe down his flank that appeared almost neon. Not the biggest fish in the river to be sure, but still a steelhead. He would be going home with me.

Time to bolt for the truck. I couldn't feel my hands or my face. The net, with the fish still in it, had frozen solid before I got there, and it seemed like the fish was well on its way to freezing as well, even though it was only thirty yards away. The fish went in the bed and I jumped into the cab and fired it up.

Do you head home after that? You could spend the rest of the day doing something that doesn't involve freezing to death. The trip was never really about enjoying a nice day on the river, it was about getting a fish, and there was a fish in the truck bed. I'll admit that I considered it. A hot cup of coffee sounded awfully good. Of course, I couldn't really do that. The sun was starting to burn through the fog, there was plenty of water left to fish and the whole day ahead of me.

It warmed up enough during the late morning and early afternoon that I could stay out and fish for an hour or so at a time before having to warm back up in the truck. When midafternoon came and the temperature began dropping again, I had had enough. No more fish had taken my fly since the first one, and the cold had taken its' toll. I headed home to greet the new year with the last fish of 2010 frozen in the bed of my truck.

From a purely technical standpoint, you can't go "winter steelheading" in eastern Washington because all of the fish are summer steelhead. A "winter" steelhead refers to something specific, a fish that enters fresh water in winter (or early spring), which you really only see closer to the coast.

So what do you call it when you're fishing for summer steelhead on a frosty day in December? Regardless of what you call it, fly fishing in freezing cold conditions is another one of those indicators that your hobby isn't just a hobby. The goal of such a trip couldn't really be said to be enjoyment or relaxation by any normal definition. All I can say is that suffering for fish either makes sense to you or it doesn't. It certainly wasn't the only time I had ever done it.

I've certainly done my share of frozen trips. Dodging icebergs on the Bighorn in February was particularly memorable. Still, I think that trip to the Tucannon was the coldest day I ever spent fly fishing. There was one day on the South Fork of the Clearwater that would be a contender. I don't know how cold it got that day either, but we weren't able to fish very effectively because the water had taken on the consistency of a slurpee.

I later heard from a friend who fishes the place regularly that the temperature on the Tucannon that last morning of 2010 had hit negative fourteen Fahrenheit. I never tried to verify that, but I guess I've chosen to believe it. Maybe if I had known that it was going to be that cold I might have thought better of going at all, or maybe not. You have to do one of those trips every now and then if only to prove to yourself that you haven't gotten old, or, God forbid, you've finally given in to being a normal, responsible adult...

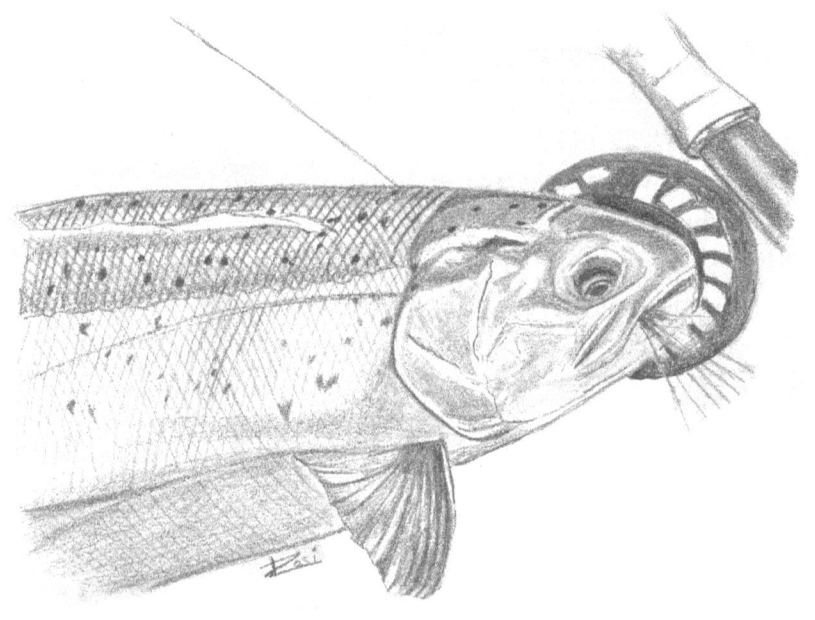

## The First Fishing Guide

You wouldn't think to look for the Bible in the sport fishing section of your local book store. Still, it does have a fish story or two. The Gospel of John, chapter 21 is about a fishing trip. Peter and several other disciples decided to go on an all-nighter on the Sea of Galilee one evening. Now I don't mean to disappoint anyone who may have gotten the impression from reading Norman Maclean that the disciples were fly fishermen, but the truth is, they were throwing nets like the rest of their contemporaries. Apparently concerns over the proper sporting ethic had not yet touched the Israeli commercial fishing industry by 33 A.D. In any case, they got skunked; and let me tell you, if you've never stayed out on a lake all night fishing only to put up a bagel, it's particularly disheartening. So morning arrives, and they see a man approaching on shore. The conversation starts out the same way it would today, with an inquiry about the fishing. We've all been there.

## The First Fishing Guide

"We didn't get anything."

There's nothing in the text about anyone adding the obligatory: "But it's just nice to be out…"

That's when things get interesting. As a fisherman, one might expect to hear any number of potential patronizing colloquialisms, such as the ever popular:

"That's why they call it fishing and not catching."

Or, if you're really lucky you'll find you've run into the local expert, who will proceed to explain to you how your particularly silly choice of techniques was the cause of your all-but-inevitable failure…

"What you need out here is a number 8 black and orange Chernobyl Hopper with a 22 CDC Blue-Winged Olive Loopwing Emerger as a dropper. My grand-daughter caught twenty yesterday on that rig. Yeah, she just turned five…"

This guy didn't go with any of the usual lines. Instead He says:

"Cast the net on the right side of the boat, and you will find some."

They followed His instructions, and when they cast out their net, they caught so many fish that they could barely drag it back in. It was at this point that they recognized that it was Jesus who was on shore. When they managed to get back in with their haul, they found that they had caught one hundred fifty-three large fish.

Now that's a fishing guide. One cast, one hundred fifty-three big ones.

In spite of the fact that Jesus was undoubtedly the world's first documented fishing guide, I don't believe that I was actually thinking about this scripture when a strange idea came to me in the winter of 2012. Somehow I got the notion that I should invite God to go fishing with me.

Now my atheist friends would probably find this particularly silly; but even believers might find the notion strange, since part of our conception of God is that he is omnipresent, making inviting him anywhere, well, redundant. Nevertheless, the idea stubbornly refused to be ignored. Besides, I really couldn't see a down-side. I didn't have any expectations about how it might affect the day's fishing, and I certainly wasn't expecting to catch one hundred fifty-three fish with a single cast. So, well, I invited The Lord to join me for a day of fly fishing for wild winter steelhead on a little stream on the Oregon coast.

No, The Creator of The Universe did not respond with a wisecrack about going after something that might actually take a fly. Sure, winter steelhead are hard to get on the fly, and considering what I went through when I first decided that I wanted to fly fish for summer steelhead, to deliberately go out looking for an even less cooperative version (and in the dead of winter, too) could be considered just a little crazy. That's kind of the point, though. I'm sure God understands…

It was mid-March, and my first winter living in western Oregon was drawing to a close. The winter steelhead season, however, was peaking. I found myself wishing I had come to the Northwest in my twenties when I would have been able to explore with a fly rod to my heart's content. All things considered, though, I got out quite a bit, and I was able to pick a "favorite" stream in time to get down to the business of learning the good holding water. My first wild winter steelhead had come to hand in that same stream in early February, a particularly well-proportioned ten pound buck. There had been a few more since then as well, and I was feeling pretty confident.

The landscape of this little steelhead stream, like so many others in the Northwest, is as striking as the fish that swim there. The coastal forest appears nearly impenetrable, rising up the face of the mountains until it disappears into the mist, parting only for the river, a blue-green stripe painted between moss-covered boulders. There always seems to be moisture in the air, even if it isn't raining. Even the smell of the place is defined by moisture; wet earth, wet evergreens, and, of course, the river itself. After twenty years of fishing up and down the Rocky Mountains, it was like another world.

That day in mid-March wasn't particularly cold, there was a layer of high clouds all day that produced nothing more than an occasional drizzle, and the water level and clarity looked just about ideal. My hopes were high. I had hit the river at just the right moment. I started the morning on a promising pool that had produced before, but no luck. The next was the same, and the one after that. So went the entire morning.

You get used to this routine with steelhead. Somewhere deep inside, the old trout fisherman still expected to come out and clobber fish all day, but the steelhead fisherman knew that putting in your time was just part of the game. Still, when you pay attention to weather patterns, water levels, and run timing, and try to schedule your trips so that you hit just about ideal conditions, you can find yourself with inflated expectations. I had allowed myself to believe that there would be steelhead in every pool…

There had to be a few fish around. I hadn't touched any of the pools upstream of my starting point, and there were definitely some good ones up there. In fact, I had what amounted to an ace up my sleeve that I had yet to play; a pool that I had already begun thinking of as "Old Reliable" because it had delivered a hook-up virtually every time I had fished it. I even came in right behind a bait fisherman once and picked up a steelhead with just a few casts. Surely it would deliver again. Or not. Even that one seemed to be empty.

Decision time. To continue upstream looking for likely holding water meant committing to a serious hike. The trail would end and it would become an exercise in fighting one's way through the brush in order to continue. Good pools were spread much thinner up there. Like I said, it required a commitment. Normally, I wouldn't go in for too much of this, preferring to fish through the more accessible areas again at the end of the day, but not this time. I just couldn't believe that the stream was empty, and it seemed like as good a time as any to explore the distant upstream runs.

Anything might be up there. Of course, I was imagining a secluded pool with a dozen large steelhead holding in plain sight. Hey, look, it's possible isn't it?

A few hours later (most of which had been spent hiking through heavy cover with a little fishing here and there), and even the possibility of stumbling across the Mother of All Honey Holes couldn't motivate me to try for just one more. The cliff I had to scale to get above an impossible run should have been enough to turn me around, but I had persevered (If that wasn't the secret gateway to Steelhead Nirvana, then what could be?). Any farther and it would just be a matter of which would run out first, the daylight or my energy. So much for hitting the peak of the run.

It was late afternoon when I made it back to Old Reliable again. A month earlier and the daylight would have been fading. At that moment, I found myself wishing it would hurry up and get dark. Leaving early has never been my m. o., but I was exhausted, a bit beat up from my adventures, and almost convinced that the river was devoid of any aquatic life forms. Then again, fishing my way back through the best runs really didn't take much more energy than just walking the last leg of the hike back to the truck. Hey, I wasn't dead, I was just tired.

Old Reliable features a two to three foot-deep fast moving riffle that drops into a very deep pool with a couple of huge boulders on the far side. The fish usually want to hold right off of those boulders. As one of the broadest (and deepest) pools on the river, with little room for a back-cast, this was one spot where I never regretted having the two-handed rod with me.

Oh yes, I was fishing a two-hander. I must have been suffering from a bit of "Spey Obsession", a malady which afflicts fly anglers here in the Northwest, sometimes for the rest of their lives. It causes one to want to fish two handed rods all the time, even in places where a one-hander would work better, like little coastal streams with lots of low-hanging trees.

Earlier the pool had appeared empty, but I was determined to fish it thoroughly before giving up for the day. After a few minutes of casting, I did something that we all most likely do on occasion, and probably innocently enough, without really thinking about what we are doing. I started bargaining.

"Lord, if I could just get *one*, I'll call it a day early and go home satisfied." I whispered under my breath.

You can probably guess what might be coming next. I hooked into a steelhead right where it should have been. It bolted downstream through a virtual mine-field of line-slicing rocks, but since I had been broken off on most of those rocks on previous trips, I pretty well knew where they all were. Let it not be said that losing fish isn't a worthwhile experience.

It was a hen of about six pounds, one of the smaller fish for that system, but I'd learned the hard way that every wild winter steelhead can whoop your butt if you don't play them right (sometimes even when you do), even the small ones. In addition to breaking me off on rocks, these fish had spit my hooks, wrapped me up on fallen logs, and snapped twelve pound tippet in mid-air. The good news was that I was becoming a better fish-player quickly as a result of the demands of my new favorite quarry. I won that battle, anyway. I admired the bright little hen as I held it by the tail; it was just beginning to show the faintest hint of pink along it's' sides. As I watched the fish disappear back into the green depths of the pool, I paused to enjoy the satisfaction of a steelhead earned with a long day on the river.

The moment didn't last. What if that fish wasn't a Karmic reward for my hard efforts that day? What if the fish were just becoming active? Should I walk away and skip the one *good* hour of fishing that I could have had after having trudged my way through nine fishless hours?

I hadn't forgotten the specifics of my situation. I had just (inadvertently) offered God a bargain, and my request appeared to have been immediately granted. I hadn't really been thinking too much about it when I did it, but there it was. But don't people do things like that all the time? He doesn't really hold us to it, does He? On the other hand, I had specifically invited Him along to spend the day on the river with me. If there was ever a time to take something like that seriously, surely this was it.

I was walking back toward the truck, only half committed to going home. The thing is, there was another primo pool only a hundred yards or so downstream. It was on the way, how much harm could it be to throw out a few lines as I walked past? Despite my misgivings, I decided that I was just being paranoid. I'm sure I had done similar things many times before and had never been struck down by lightning bolts from the sky.

I came to the next run, where a shallow riffle flows into a nice medium-depth pool with walking speed current. The one little issue with this spot; tree branches that hang out over the river through all of the best holding water. A (back-handed) side-arm cast up under the trees is needed here. Now, contrary to popular belief, you can cast a Spey rod one-handed; and as long as you don't need your casting arm for anything important for the next twenty-four hours or so, and you brought some ibuprofen for the drive home, you could even do it all day. I made my first cast into the riffle; if there was a fish right at the drop-off, this would put a fly in front of it. My line stopped before it made it into the pool, and I lifted the rod to find myself snagged on the bottom. I was still well above the best holding water, so I decided to wade out a bit and try to get a better angle and free my line. It was no use, and I ended up leaving my fly and tippet on the river bottom.

Whether a break-off at a time like that is just an especially annoying turn of events or a well-timed que to pack it in depends mostly on your state of mind. Sure I was heading back, but reeling up and walking right past some of the best water in the river; well, that was not the plan. How would I know if there was an active fish holding in this pool as well? It could be one of the really nice ones…

If it occurred to me that losing my entire set-up on my first cast was a gentle nudge from The Almighty that I was supposed to "go home satisfied", I quickly buried the thought. I stayed where I was and tied everything back up, then prepared to cast out again. I worked out some line and brought my rod up to set up a roll cast. To my horror, I felt the rod smack against branches as it came up to the vertical position. I had inadvertently waded out to the point where the longest branches of the tree were overhead, and in my state of irritated distraction I hadn't noticed. I looked up to see my fly, leader, and even my fly line itself in a horrifying tangle in the tree. I was so stunned by my own carelessness that I couldn't even manage to be angry. I just stared at the mess of line wrapped around every (#@!!%*) branch in the tree with a dumbfounded look on my face.

My attempts to free the line were completely futile. I had to resort to brute force, leaning my weight against the line and hoping for a break in the leader or tippet, but the tangle could not be defeated. The fly line snapped. Once again I was left staring dumfounded, this time at what was left of my fly line. That was enough. I reeled in and headed toward the truck feeling a bit shell-shocked. In all my years of fly fishing I had never broken a fly line, much less by hanging it up in a tree.

So, losing a compact Scandi shooting head to a low hanging tree isn't exactly a classic example of the Wrath of God. One usually imagines plagues or brimstone from the sky when pondering such things. Nevertheless, I had to at least consider the possibility that I had actually experienced a correction from The Lord. Mind you, I'm not the guy who sees divine intervention in every little thing, either. I can't say for sure that the World's First Fishing Guide put me on that steelhead, or that I got a slap on the wrist for bargaining with God and then immediately blowing off my end of the bargain. I'm sure I've done similar things many times and never noticed anything that appeared like punishment from above. Still, there was the invitation. That was a first. Maybe it was a coincidence, you can take what you will from the story, but it got my attention anyway.

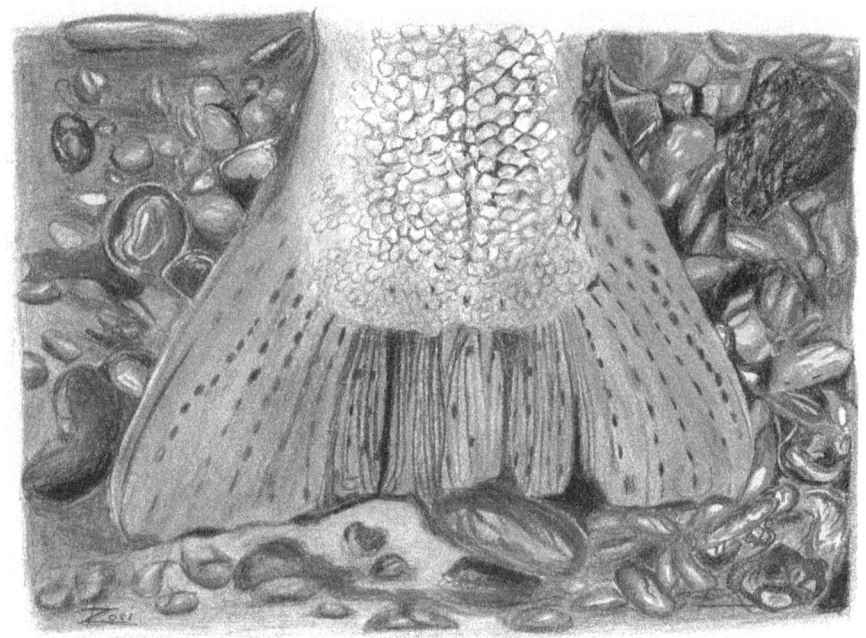

## (Teeny) Footprints in the Sand

"Where are you?!!?!!" I yelled at the television.

Now I normally don't shout at the television; with the possible exception of a goal-line fumble in a playoff game. Nevertheless, there I was, coming unglued as I watched the twentieth anniversary edition of Jim Teeny's *Catching More Steelhead* video. He was sight-casting to huge summer steelhead and clobbering them one after another. The beast he was hoisting from the water as I went semi-berserk looked like it would weigh in at around eighteen pounds.

"That doesn't happen!!! There's nowhere where you can do that!" I shouted.

The fish were all sitting in (more or less) plain sight, and he was able to get close to them and place precision casts (with Teeny Nymphs, of course) right in their faces. The rivers were moderately sized, and the water was crystal clear. I'd started steelhead fishing about seven years earlier after moving from Colorado to eastern Washington and had never experienced anything like that. I was about ready to peel off my own skin watching him do it again and again; and, of course, the fish were gorgeous.

Another move had recently brought me to Newberg, Oregon, which meant I was in the market for a few streams that I could get to know well. I knew Teeny lived near Portland, in fact he was scheduled to give a presentation at my favorite local fly shop in the immediate future. If those were his home waters, which seemed likely to me, then they were probably nearby.

Of course, most of what you hear from the previous generation of fishermen is how steelheading in the U.S. is no more than a pale shadow of what it once was, and anyone under sixty was just born too late. With that in mind, I had to consider the possibility that the quality of fishing that the movie portrayed from more than twenty years earlier might no longer exist. Nevertheless, I became determined to find and fish the rivers from the film.

Jim Teeny turned out to be a very nice, personable guy. Though he hadn't come to give a presentation on a video he made twenty five years earlier, he was willing to answer questions. As I suspected, all of the rivers from the video were located in either northern Oregon or south-western Washington. I had some names and potential destinations; all I had to do was wait for the right time of year. I chose a destination in Washington for my first attempt, which came in the early summer, at what I thought would be a good time. I went out with high hopes.

For some adventurous souls, fishing can become the Quest for the Unattainable, The Holy Grail if you will; a spot that offers fishing so good that nothing better could ever be found, and so the search could only be called off should one actually find such a place. If you fall into this group then this eternal quest becomes so integral to your experience that you can actually come to fear finding what you are looking for. As much as you would get to enjoy the fishing (ostensibly for the rest of your life), was it not the search itself that was so compelling? Was it not the belief, without certainty, that such a place exists, and could be discovered by the pure of heart that caused each trip to a new river to hold the anticipation of a child on Christmas morning? To find it in a way that felt like it was too quick or too easy would leave you feeling cheated, even if you had been looking for twenty years.

As unlikely as it may have seemed, I actually found myself nervous that I might be about to stumble across such a place. Sight fishing for pods of twenty pound summer steelhead at close range and having it work; and all of this close to home? I was wondering if I would be making the call to my brother later that night to let him know that I had found The Grail…

Steelhead fishing is still steelhead fishing no matter what you think you know, which means no guarantees. I understood that, but I was still a little disappointed when my first attempt at replicating what I had seen in Jim Teeny's video ended without a single fish being spotted, much less caught. That early summer trip turned out to be an exercise in hiking around a boulder-strewn stream all day. It was a beautiful spot, like they all seem to be in the Northwest, and I figured at the time that I would be back to try again soon.

Fly fishing can become a very single-minded pursuit at times. A single species can be the target of all of your efforts, almost to the point of (dare I say it?) obsession. The "in thing" these days, though, seems to be the conquest of many species with the fly rod; that theme seems to run through the collective consciousness of fly fishing wherever you look. It's as if there was a virtual checklist of species and places that one needs to tick off if one expects to be a self-actualized fly fisherman. Still, with so much fishing near home it almost seems a waste to wander off when you haven't covered your own backyard in anything approaching a complete way.

The point is that I had another agenda besides just my desire to re-enact Jim Teeny's exploits from the video. I wanted to expand my checklist of species, but my target was a local fish, and arguably the mightiest creature you can catch on a fly rod in fresh water; the Chinook salmon. Fishing for Fall Chinook will compete for your time if you also want to hit the fall hot spots for summer steelhead. At least for that particular year, I decided that there would be plenty of steelhead (big steelhead) around in winter.

Try talking to people about fly fishing for Chinook and you're likely to hear widely varying points of view on the topic. Some people just look at you like you've got a screw loose if you mention the idea. "I'm sorry to hear that" was one response I heard when I told a tackle-shop salmon guru that I was going to fish for them with a fly rod rather that bait-casting gear. Others say that it is not only doable, but can be very effective under the right conditions. I knew it was possible to hook a Chinook on a fly because I had done it, though I had yet to land one.

The first time was the previous fall. I had gone to explore new reaches of a stream in southwestern Washington that I had fished on several previous occasions in hopes of finding steelhead. I was armed with what was my favorite steelhead rod at the time, my ten-foot seven-weight.

I was determined to explore some canyon water that morning, and on this particular river, canyon means *Canyon*. I actually rappelled down to the river using a rope that was no doubt left by some regulars for just that purpose. The first pool I came to was deep and slow moving. From the rocky ledges of the bank I could look down into the perfectly clear water and see what was clearly a pod of salmon holding near the bottom.

I looked back at the cliff I had just come down and briefly considered climbing back up and grabbing my nine-weight, but quickly dismissed the idea. Besides the potential heart attack I might suffer from an extra trip up and back down, it seemed unlikely that they would take a fly, so why bother? Besides, were I to actually hook one, I figured I could handle it on the seven.

In my attempt to verify for myself that they would not take a fly, I proceeded to hook (and lose) three Chum salmon. They all appeared to be in the ten pound range, and now my interest was piqued.

I continued to explore. The next pool downstream was more traditional steelhead water; a broader, shallower run full of rocks and broken currents. I found a fish holding behind one of the larger rocks, in a perfect steelhead lie. It was happy to grab my streamer on the first pass, and then proceeded to do everything it could to hog-tie me in my own fly line. It bolted for the far bank, hurling itself so high into the air and so close to shore that I thought it might beach itself. Then it sprinted back at me, passing on the upstream side and turned downstream again, all within a few seconds, leaving me spinning in my precarious position on a bed of slippery rocks. That fish deserved to get off, but somehow I managed to land it. You've gotta love steelhead.

As a steelheader, and particularly a fly fisherman, any time you catch fish you ought to consider it a good day. I had a nice hatchery steelhead in the cooler before noon, so, by definition, it was a good day. But it wasn't over just yet.

The next pod of fish I came across appeared to be a group of Chinook. They looked too big to be anything else. Again I thought about switching to the nine-weight. A heavier leader would be a good idea as well. The fish were *awfully* large, but I'd just waded into position, and I just wanted to *see* if one would take a fly. I didn't expect it to work. I'd just make a few casts with what I had…

The pool was moderately sized, but deep, with a large boulder breaking the current in the middle. The fish were moving around, but they seemed to want to congregate behind the rock.

I had to work the pool for a while, trying to get a fly to run through the water behind the rock just right. The one that finally took was big. When it felt the sting of the hook it came up and gave a tremendous thrash on the surface and broke my line like it was no more substantial than a spider web.

From that one look I guessed the fish was over twenty pounds, maybe over thirty. It would have been my first Chinook on a fly rod.

My sense of personal justice required me to kick myself. Maybe the result would have been the same either way, maybe not, but it sure seemed stupid at that moment to have blown off gearing up with something heavier. I could have landed that fish...

Still, you can only get so upset with yourself when you've just had an epiphany. I may have blown my chance for the time being, but I had discovered for myself the truth of the matter; Chinook will take a fly (and not just on remote streams in Alaska). I promised myself I would plan a trip for the next fall to that same river at the peak of the run.

Now next year had come, and it was time to make the trip back to that same stream in southwestern Washington, which, incidentally, was also one that was on Jim Teeny's list from the movie. I wasn't thinking so much about sight casting for steelhead, though I hadn't exactly forgotten about it either.

It was late September, but you'd have never known it from the weather. It was a bright, sunny day and almost warm enough to fool one into thinking it was mid-summer. I started on a broad, riffly pool in the lower river. There were plenty of Chinook around, but none of them seemed to want to strike. They were right there, I was getting my fly in front of them, but... nothing. I tried an arsenal of flies with the same result until I had burned up the entire morning.

Puzzled and a bit disheartened, I decided to try the canyon section. Perhaps the salmon wouldn't be up so high, and I could stalk a steelhead or two. I ventured higher than I had gone before, to one of the deepest parts of the canyon. I hiked down the trail to the river and found a run that seemed strangely broad for one so high up in the system. A small rapid gave way to a broad stretch of riffled current that could (and did) hold a lot of fish. It looked like a great place for steelhead, except that it was full of Chinook. They were literally everywhere, and even though I had spent my entire morning in a futile effort to entice a take from essentially the same fish, it's awfully hard to resist casting to big fish when they're right in front of you.

I started with a black size 4 Motion Prawn, a fly that I thought might be interesting to a salmon or a steelhead, and it didn't take long to find out. There was a fish in plain sight and (reasonably) shallow water where a fly could be presented well, and he took it almost right away.

I had learned my lesson the previous year. Fish had slipped my hooks and broken my leaders. Not this time. This time I was loaded for bear. Well, Chinook salmon, anyway. I had my nine-weight Sage, my Ross big game reel, and twenty pound leader. I swung my rod downstream and slammed the hook home.

There was no mistaking the powerful head shakes, I had one on! The fish took off, peeling line off my reel with ease. I had my drag set tight, but it didn't seem to notice. It made a lap around the pool before coming back in close to start a bull-dogging battle that seemed to go on and on. The fight wasn't as exciting as a steelhead, but the sheer strength of the salmon was impressive. This thing was the aquatic equivalent of a fullback with a twenty-two inch neck. I'm not sure how much time went by as I applied constant, heavy side pressure and still its head wouldn't turn. I finally managed to bring in the fifteen pound buck, and it was in pretty good shape.

I'd watched the fish take the fly, yet somehow I wasn't fully satisfied until I saw my black Motion Prawn buried perfectly in the scissors of its jaw. Perfection. My mission was accomplished.

Mission accomplished or not, there was still plenty of daylight left and plenty of fish. The pool above the rapid was deeper and slower, and the fish, of which there were several, were busily swimming around in circles. It wasn't exactly the perfect place to present a fly, but I tried for a bit anyway, switching to the most visible, most obnoxious, four-inch-long pink streamer I had.

Predictably, the preoccupied fish ignored my offerings, but as I walked away I spotted something just ahead of the tailout the pool. It

*(Teeny) Footprints in the Sand*

appeared to be a small Chinook in a shallow trough not more than fifteen feet from me, and I could see it clearly. What's more, it was in a spot that could be targeted easily with a fly. A good cast could force the fish to either bite or move. I figured it would choose the latter and swim off after one cast, but I had to give it a shot.

The first cast missed the mark by just a hair. The fly drifted just over the fish, and it moved slightly to avoid it, but it didn't spook. Okay, time to get serious. I cast a bit farther upstream, and let the fly sink and dead drift down toward the fish. I gave it a twitch. Wow, that thing looks alive, like a little squid; then I let it swing a bit, then drift, another twitch, swing just a hair, drift… it's going right into his face, he's not moving out of the way… chomp!

It bit down broadside on the fly like a Great White hitting a seal. Pink marabou was hanging out of both sides of its mouth.

After a moment of shock I set the hook hard and the fish took off like a rocket downstream. Into the air it went as it hurtled through the small rapid and into the next pool. This fish had explosive energy, and was ripping downstream against a rig that was set for something three times its' size.

How was it doing that? It just wasn't that big. It jumped again. Did I see a pink stripe? Wait a minute… a steelhead? All of a sudden it made sense. After a few more nice runs and another jump or two the fish came into view as I slowly gained ground. It was a steelhead of about eight pounds.

What a battle! Somehow, steelhead never cease to surprise me.

It didn't occur to me until I was on the road headed home that I had accomplished both of my goals that day. I got my first Chinook on a fly, and I got to sight cast to a steelhead and watch the take. It had been a good day, though the Quest for The Grail was by no means over. The river I had fished was one of Jim Teeny's favorite streams; and though I didn't know it well enough to recognize particular spots from the film, for all I knew I may have been walking in his very footsteps. Cool.

There was something else that had been floating around in the back of my mind since the whole Jim Teeny thing began. It was an image of a distinctive looking man holding a big, dark, mean-looking Chinook in a small stream against a snowy background. The man seemed familiar, though I couldn't recall ever knowing who it was. That image was stuck in my mind because it was the cover of the first fishing magazine I ever bought. It was late 1993, and as a newcomer to fly fishing I can remember looking at the cover of that magazine (*Fly Fisherman,* December 1993) and thinking: "You can catch *that* on a fly rod??!?!!"

Being a bit of a pack rat and a natural collector to boot, I saved it, along with just about all of the others I ever read. It would be packed away in the garage, so I could check to see if my suspicion was correct. You see, I had seen that man's picture here and there in fishing publications over the years without actually taking the time to figure out who it was. By the time I met the man himself, he was much older, and I had other things on my mind. I dug that old magazine out, and sure enough, it was Jim Teeny, there on the cover of the first fly fishing magazine I ever bought; and the article, which I probably read in the living room of my apartment in Tucson, Arizona nineteen years earlier, was about fly fishing for salmon in the very river I had just come from.

At times like that all one can do is raise an eyebrow and offer one's best impression of Mr. Spock: "Fascinating…"

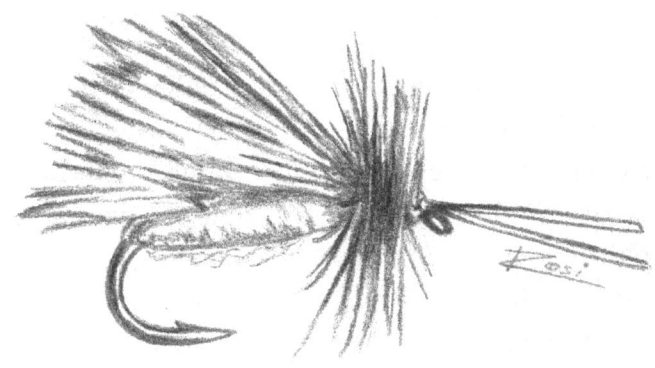

## Night of the Grass-Popper

Part of me was concerned. The sun was going down, I still hadn't arrived at my destination, a little campground on a favorite Northwestern trout stream, and I really wanted to throw out a few lines before it got dark. I also needed to set up the tent, which really requires two people to erect, by myself and do it quickly. It would be that much harder in the dark. On the other hand, there was another part of me that knew exactly how things would turn out.

You see, over the years I have come to realize that I have supernatural powers. No, really, just bear with me for a minute. In this case, it consists of the ability to arrive at any destination, regardless of distance, travel time, mode of transportation, weather conditions, etc. at the last possible second.

Okay, so supernatural punctuality isn't as exciting as say, telekinesis, but hey, what were you expecting? It really does seem to happen all the time, and it's not because I necessarily plan it that way. I can have an 11:00 AM appointment on the other side of the state, and I won't show up at 10:59 or 11:01. It'll be 11:00:00. It has a certain creepiness factor...

Now I suppose you could look at this either as the habit of always being precisely on time or perpetually almost late. The up side is that I tend to end up wasting very little of my life waiting around because I have arrived somewhere irrationally early. It's a bit of a pain in the behind in situations like the one in which I currently found myself, though. I'd been in the truck for eight hours, and there I was, barreling down the last few miles of winding canyon road as the sun was setting.

I hesitated only for a moment after pounding the last tent stake. The sun had set. The two other people in the campground had finished their fishing days. The one who appeared about my age (forty-something) was just settling in for some relaxation around the fire. The other, a much older gentleman, appeared to have already gone to bed. I could get a fire going, settle in, maybe get to sleep early, and be ready to go first thing in the morning. That would be the sensible thing to do.

Right. Maybe if my "trout on a dry fly" jones hadn't been quite so overwhelming at that moment I would have. You see, recent moves had taken me away from the "close-to-trout-streams" lifestyle I had lived for so many years in and around the Rocky Mountains (don't feel too sorry for me, I'm close to salmon and steelhead now). In fact, my last really good outing for trout had been three and a half years earlier, at the same river that was now flowing past no more than thirty yards from where I stood, gently gurgling and splashing in the background, beckoning me like the aroma of fresh brewed coffee on a rainy Sunday morning. Sure I had been mentally preparing myself over the eight hours in the truck for having to wait until the next morning to fish; I tried to accept the idea that I would be lucky to not end up fumbling around in the dark with the tent; but that was because I realized that the actual odds of arriving at the precise minute in a twenty-four hour period that would give me exactly enough time to set up the tent, wader up, rig up my four-weight, and get down to the water in time to get one fish were approximately .07%. Well, that's what they would be for someone without my "power".

Hell yes I got rigged up and got down to the water, and yes, it was all but completely dark. It had been a few years since I'd fished that stretch of river, but sometimes stepping out of the world and into a trout stream can seem a bit like stepping out of time as well. Watching that high-riding dry fly drift downstream against the last light of day reflecting off the surface of the water, it was like I'd never left. At times like that you can almost see your whole life as an unbroken series of fishing trips.

I didn't have much time for feeling nostalgic just then, though. It took just a few casts to coax a beautiful nineteen inch brown to rise to my size sixteen yellow humpy. I had my reward, and as the last light faded to black I made my way back to camp feeling pretty satisfied, but somehow not surprised. Absolute. Last. Possible. Second.

Of course, this trip was about more than trying to see if I could spend eight hours in a truck for the sake of catching a single fish four hundred and thirty miles from home before the sun went down. It was actually something of a reunion. My brother Chris and my oldest friend Clayton Nelson would be arriving the next afternoon to join me. "The Pack", as the three of us called ourselves as young children, had been inseparable throughout the second half of the seventies and much of the eighties. Yes, I know we had the least creative name any group of childhood friends ever came up with. I think my Dad and his little gang back in the 1930s / 1940s called themselves "The Seven Aces". Sure, it sounds hokey when you've grown up, but at least they put some effort into it…

Anyway, we grew up a block apart and had been friends since kindergarten. We also learned the ways of the fly rod together in the early 1990s, and shared some memorable adventures before we all went our separate ways after college. All of that connection made it strange to think that we had let nineteen years go by since the last time the three of us fished together.

My job the next morning was to prospect and have something to report for my companions when they arrived. It was early October, and though this little stream had been a favorite of mine for the few years that I spent within (reasonable) striking distance of its' inviting waters, I had never been there in the fall. We were warned that we would encounter low water and spooky fish. As much as I enjoyed fishing the predictable hatches of summer, that actually sounded great.

The fishing was exactly as foretold, with the need for tiny flies and 7x tippet being the rule. In the light of day, that size sixteen humpy would have been an excellent choice for putting down every fish in the river. The most effective pattern was more like a size twenty-two Parachute Adams. It was maddening at times; anything other than a 110% perfect drift would draw a refusal. Of course, that made it all the more satisfying when you fooled one.

I spent the morning unable to tear myself away from a pod of surface feeding rainbows, even after I had determined that they were all a bit on the small side. There's just something about fish rising right in front of you. What's that old saying about a bird in hand? Then again, if I just wanted a trout in hand I could go to the grocery store and buy one, and skip the 900 mile drive, so that can't be it.

It wasn't what I had come for, but at least I managed to pick up a half dozen moderate sized rainbows by noon. Well, there was one big brown. I spotted him on the way out just before lunch. He was a colorful twenty inch male in a particularly tricky spot. That made my morning. So… six little rainbows to hand *does not* beat one big brown under a bush, or something to that effect.

My companions arrived in mid-afternoon. After the requisite one-arm man-hug / chest bumps had been exchanged we headed for the river. I suggested we go downstream, but we had to pass by the same pool where I had spent the morning, and damned if we weren't all drawn in by the Siren song of that same pod of rising fish. I warned everyone that they were mostly smaller rainbows, not the big browns we had come for, but they were right there, beckoning us with their rhythmically rising noses…

Of course it wasn't a total loss, how could it be? Besides, it turned out there was one big rainbow in there with all of those little fish, though he took quite a bit of coaxing, and the low light of dusk helped as well. Clay found a twenty inch brown of his own, and Chris picked up some good fish too, though when we got back to camp and popped open the first of our "fishing trip beers", this one an Oregonian brew called *20" Brown,* I felt it was my duty to give him a hard time. We didn't pick that beer by accident, so of course you're going to razz the guy who didn't get the big one that day…

On the topic of measuring fish; well I suppose I would have to say that the practice gets a lot of undue criticism. It conjures the specter of competition (which is frowned upon in fly fishing circles, you know…), or even poorly understood concepts in Freudian psychoanalysis. Neither insecurity nor an overly competitive nature are necessary to be interested in such information. I often measure fish, generally for no more complicated reason than curiosity. I suppose I also like to keep my eye calibrated. There was a time when my companions and I may have been competitive about who caught the biggest fish, but that time passed long ago. Still, when your eye is well calibrated, you realize just how much folks tend to exaggerate the size of fish they've caught. I once had a guide show me pictures of a little girl long-arming a sixteen inch rainbow and tell me: "That there is a ten pound rainbow. That's what we catch out there…" The strangest part was his expectation of being believed. It becomes easy to understand how fishermen have acquired a reputation as compulsive liars.

Don't get me wrong. I consider this little gap of understanding between myself and other fly fishermen to be entirely my fault. I have learned over the years that many things that I, in the foolishness of my youth, considered to be virtues, turn out to be, in general company, little more than annoying character flaws that I simply can't seem to grow out of; a preference for the conveying of accurate information being one of these.

In any case, suffice it to say that if you figure that an exaggeration of 10% is normal, you should probably adjust that up to somewhere between 30% and 50%. I can't tell you how many fish pictures I've been shown where someone swore the fish was two feet long, and all I could think was "Sure, as long as the person holding that seventeen inch fish is Andre the Giant's twin brother." I guess in the end I like to keep myself honest, too.

Few things will get me feeling nostalgic like thinking back to our fly fishing trips from college, when our campground fare was Keystone Light and canned chili. Nevertheless, at some point my brother Chris and I decided that we should combine the things we loved, like great food and great wine with trout streams and camping. Over the years we took this routine about as far as we could. Of course, you can catch a few confused stares from other campers who are happily mowing down hot dogs and Budweiser when you are enjoying sautéed foie gras and Sauternes in the next campground.

So, we got a little carried away. Hell, we probably could've starred in our own Food Network show. Perhaps instead of *The Property Brothers*, we could have been *The Prime-Grade Beef Brothers* (yes, we are twins), and spent half the show debating the relative merits of the ribeye versus the New York strip. Then, while tantalizing the audience with the sights and sounds of well-marbled steaks sizzling on the grill, we could proceed to argue about whether a 1997 Joseph Phelps Insignia was the ultimate wine to accompany such a feast, or if we should go with the 1996 Opus One. Wait, this sounds too much like an episode of *Frasier*.

Okay, since we're talking about a Food Network show, maybe we would have had a catchy name like *The Campground Gourmet*. Either way, we went all out for this trip, sans a re-enactment of Niles and Frasier Crane arguing about vintages.

"Coming up next on *The Campground Gourmet*... Boom! Prime grade ribeyes seared to a perfect medium rare, mashed potatoes, steamed asparagus in a lemon butter sauce, and a beautiful Sonoma Coast Pinot Noir, all served camp-fireside on the banks of a world-class trout stream! Oh, and later on folks, we're gonna sip some small-batch bourbon around the fire; you're not gonna want to miss this, so don't go away!" Yeah, that's how we roll...

We awoke the next morning to a beautiful autumn day. Okay, technically, we skipped the early morning fishing as a result of staying up too late the night before, but it was freezing early in the morning, so that was okay with us. So anyway, after the morning chill burned off, it was beautiful. We had clear skies and temperatures in the sixties. That's just about my idea of perfection.

The river flows through a desert landscape, but with spectacular cliffs and rock formations lending to the distinctively western scenery, one could end up spending the whole day just looking around. After fly fishing for trout in desert rivers for twenty years, I guess it shouldn't seem strange to me anymore. Still, as pretty as the scenery may be, sometimes when I'm out at one of these places where man-made dams have created a trout paradise in a place where they might not even survive naturally, I catch myself thinking: "Really? Shouldn't there be a pine tree or two around?"

Inland flats stalking. That's the best way I can come up with to describe the fishing. Let's just say that it doesn't suck. In fact, I can think of very few things in fly fishing that are more satisfying than spotting a big brown trout cruising through a glassy pool, dropping a dry fly as delicately as you can right in his path, and watching him come up and casually take it, never suspecting that in the next instant that his tasty morsel would be trying to drag him out of the water.

Chris and I spent the day targeting those super-finicky fish with our microscopic dry flies, but I lost track of Clay. I couldn't tell what he was throwing at them, but it seemed like he was tinkering with different approaches to fooling them.

The end of the day found us fishing a small pool with just enough room for the three of us. By the time the sun set I had exhausted the supply of feeding trout in front of me, and had somehow managed to put a nice tangle in my leader. It was getting dark quickly, and the temperature was dropping at about the same pace. Reeling up, I walked over toward Clay, just in time to see him cast out a foamy, high-riding dry fly that was big enough to be seen clearly from space (at least compared to the twenty-twos I was using), and start stripping it in aggressively. Whatever it was, he was fishing it a bit like a surface popper, like we had once done for bass back in Arizona.

"There's no way that's gonna…" I started to say, just in time to look over and see a fish explode on the fly, very much like a largemouth would have.

Sadly, the fight was over before it started, as the fish had broken the light line on the take.

"What did you have on there?" I asked.

"Hopper." Clay responded.

"You have to try that again." I replied.

I fumbled around in my vest until I found my hat-light, which is somehow never where I think I left it, and usually has dead batteries when I need it most. At least this one time, I had thought to change them out before the trip. Chris walked over as Clay was tying on a new hopper. We both wanted to see Act II, and it didn't take long. Clay cast out again, and began stripping/popping. The fish came back with another ferocious strike, but this time it missed.

"Oooh!!!" Chris and I yelled simultaneously, in our best "dropped pass in the corner of the end-zone" voices.

A few more attempts produced one more strike, and again the fish missed the fly. Sadly, we had to admit it was just too dark to go on at some point (okay, the fish had stopped coming up, and so it was too dark). The fish would remain a mystery.

Just what was the unseen assailant of Clay's Grass-popper? Well, left to the imagination, what could it be but a nine-pound brown with jaws like an alligator? That's the stuff of fish stories, is it not? Then we had to go and kill the romance by fishing the next run downstream the following morning, where Clay hooked a fish that had the same hopper pattern lodged in its jaw. I guess it's always kind of cool to get a fly back from a fish that broke you off, but it wasn't quite the Fish of Legend that we might have imagined. Still, it's hard to be disappointed with an average fish when they're as nice as they are out there.

That's fishing for you. That fish that broke you off that you never saw; the one that haunts you for years to come and gets bigger each time you tell the story... you know the one. Every now and then remember to stop and be thankful for those, because they might have turned out to be just another average fish had you managed to land them; and legends aren't made of such as that, but of the ghosts of the river that can never truly be caught.

Oh yeah, there's one more thing. Clay hooked up with a big brown just before we had to leave. It snapped his 7x with a final burst of energy right in front of the net. No imagination necessary; we saw it up close and personal and it was probably the best fish of the trip, so he's going to be haunted after all. Like I said, that's fishing for you.

## Cursed

I have a confession. I have never caught a Deschutes River steelhead. It's true. I can hear the distant sounds of torches being lit and angry villagers grabbing their pitchforks, but before you string me up, Doc, let me explain.

I don't make it over to the Deschutes very often. I have plenty of good excuses for this. It's a two-and-a-half hour drive from my home in Newberg to the mouth of the river. There are certainly closer places. I also have a family at home, so there are plenty of times when I just can't get out at all. But the real reason that I've stayed away for several years is that I'm cursed. Don't get me wrong. I'm not superstitious per se. I don't make sure to eat chicken before each fishing trip, for example, or ask Jobu to come and "take fear from fly rods" when I find myself in a slump.

Now anyone who has ever cast a line into any sort of moisture knows what I'm talking about. Curses are just part of the game. It could be as simple as getting nary so much as a nibble while everyone around you is catchin' 'em like gangbusters, even the three-year-old kid who's fishing in a rain puddle with ¾ inch rope tied to an old golf club. Or it could be something really bad.

This particular curse prevents me from ever catching a steelhead from the Deschutes. I have no idea if there is an escape clause, though I believe that it is traditional to have one. If so, there is no way to know if I need to kiss a frog, or have someone fit me for a glass wading boot, or maybe draw a magical fly rod from a stone (I like the sound of that one…).

What's more, there is an impressive level of scientific literacy involved. After observing the reaction of the river's trout population to my flies, I can only assume that the curse-crafting fiend thought to use the term Oncorhynchus mykiss rather than the common name of steelhead. Even during a stonefly hatch, it was like offering Panda burgers at a P.E.T.A. convention. As much as it may seem particularly malicious, you have to admire the attention to detail.

When you've observed conclusive evidence that supernatural forces have aligned to prevent you from catching fish, you'd think that the impression would stick with you. But time can make one question anything. When looked at through the hazy perspective of hindsight, even a fishing trip so chocked full of inexplicable disasters as to make Murphy himself shake his head in disbelief can be dismissed as a random series of coincidences.

Then one day you start talking to a fly shop guy who says he does day trips over there regularly, and has been killin' 'em the last few weeks. He doesn't even get up early. He hits the river starting in late morning and kicks piscatorial posteriors 'til the sun goes down. That sounds pretty good. You start dreaming about aggressive steelies grabbing your swung fly and virtually pulling the rod out of your hands.

Curses aren't real. So, your (lifetime) tally of flat tires at the Deschutes is higher than your tally of fish caught. Coincidence. And maybe it's a *little* odd that, based on your past experience, you are statistically more likely to have your tent blown away in a wind storm than you are to hook a fish. That's just paranoia talking. Besides that, knowing that you are the only fisherman in the Northwest who has never beached a steelie from the D kinda sucks. I was going back…

Despite my efforts, September escaped without a steelhead coming to hand. I didn't think much of it, it's steelheading after all. I only made it out one day in the middle of the month, and it went by without any unnatural disasters. Conditions were tough, mostly due to the off-color water that seemed to plague the river throughout 2015. That this would coincide with my return didn't strike me as odd at all. If I were to consider this part of The Curse, I would then have to concede that it's tentacles extend to my entire fishing experience. For example, I hardly notice that when I finally get around to fishing the Coho run on another well-known local river, which has had strong returns for thousands of years, the run mysteriously dies. I just assume it's like that for everyone…

The destruction of my Scandi shooting head by means of, shall we say, an "unusual" accident didn't go by quite so unnoticed. All I was doing was a little tackle maintenance the night before a trip in early October. My attempt to unravel what appeared to be nothing more than a perfectly ordinary, perfectly natural (horrific) tangle somehow ended with the tippet cinching down on the center of the fly line and slicing it through down to the core. Though not conclusively supernatural, it still struck me as at least a bit odd; kind of like the key witness in a Mafia king-pin trial dying by accidental strangulation with a curtain cord. You don't need to be Columbo to find it suspicious…

On a side note, I have on several occasions inquired of my Dear Old Dad as to why he didn't have the decency to pass along to me the proper genetic codes for his height, not to mention his oversized hands and forearms, with which I am certain I could have thrown a football one hundred yards or hit a baseball six hundred feet. He has been kind enough to remind me on such occasions that were I nothing more than an exact clone, I would also have his poor hearing and vision, making the chances of being able to hit a ninety-mile-an-hour slider rather low. What I did get from him are certain personality traits, including the irresistible urge to unleash strings of expletives upon unsuspecting inanimate objects. I certainly could not abide such an affront to decency on the part of a fly line; at least not without letting it know what a no-good, rat-bastard piece-of-crap S.O.B. it really was.

In retrospect, maybe it wasn't the best idea to go ahead and finish loading my gear in the truck while still foaming at the mouth. It made sense at the time. I felt like throwing things; I just had to aim for the truck.

I awoke the next morning to an overwhelming sense of impending doom. In my experience the first mishap of a fishing trip is never the last. It's more like the first cough of Tuberculosis. My little voice was telling me to skip the whole thing. Stay home, let the dark cloud pass, and go fishing another day.

When I arrived at the river I was calm and focused. Of course I went fishing. Like I would ever listen to the second half of a sentence that started with: "Don't go fishing today". Little voice... pffff. I'd managed through sheer force of will to set aside my apprehension. I'd also stopped and picked up a new Scandi shooting head on the way out, so I was good to go.

It was a beautiful day. The sun was out, the temperature was perfect, and all was right with the world. There were still a few hardy souls camping in the campground near the mouth of the river. Several fishermen were about, and some were even returning with fish. I sat there taking it all in just long enough to scarf down the lunch I had packed.

Time to gear up. I started with the rod and reel, as is my habit when it isn't raining. Then the waders. I heard a faint, distant noise that I'd swear was a low, sinister laugh riding on the wind. Wait, somehow I can't remember grabbing them... No, no, no... I felt the icy hand of Doom on my shoulder as I went to pop the seat forward to grab my waders. In the split second between going for the seat and actually seeing the empty spot where they should have been, I knew I had forgotten them.

Five hours of driving. Five (#%&**!#!!) hours. For nothing. Flashing images of myself going berserk with a broadsword in a crowded shopping mall blurred my vision as I calmly went through the motions of double checking everywhere to confirm that they weren't there; but, in a way, I was almost relieved. Compared to the metaphysical pummelings I had taken on some of my previous outings, a simple waste of time and effort was relatively mild. The other shoe dropping could have been anything, up to and including a twelve ton boulder rolling off a cliff and squashing me just as I was about to land that first glorious steelhead.

The way I saw it, I had three options. I could drive to the fly shop in Hood River and buy the cheapest pair of waders that a super-premium fly shop would have in stock, and then drive back and fish the last few hours of daylight. I decided to save that one for when I might *want* to get divorced. Option two was wet wading. In October. In sweat pants. I packed everything up and began the drive home.

Two and a half hours is a long time to stew in your own juices. I racked my brain trying to remember a time when I had made it all the way to a river only to have to turn back for having forgotten a key piece of gear. In better than twenty years of this routine, I couldn't remember a single one. Don't get me wrong, I'd forgotten things before. I'd just always found a way out. Forgot to grab the wading boots? Well, my hiking boots were pretty darn tight over waders, and they didn't last long after that day, but I still fished. I even forgot my *reel* once, and I still found a way to fish; but that's a story for another time.

I could always try it again the next day. All I would have to do would be to throw my waders in the truck and I'd be ready. The thought caught me off-guard at first. Seriously? The hell with this place, the hell with this drive! I have other things to do anyway. What the hell? Was it really too much to expect that I could actually have a successful outing to the Deschutes? Apparently so. A disaster every time. The hell with it.

Of course I went back the next day. If nothing else, I knew I would be grumpy until I had a chance to redeem myself. Why put my family through that? Besides, how long could a streak of bad luck last?

So there I was, rolling east along highway 84 when the Columbia River came into view. For those who may have never seen it, the Columbia is a colossus of a river. At a mile across, you'd think it was a lake; except on days when it looks more like the ocean, complete with three to four foot white-capped swells. Uh-oh. Then I noticed the trees. Then I felt my five thousand pound truck getting blown off course.

Gale-force winds. Haven't we done that one before? Where's the creativity, the originality? How about this: the world's first freshwater steelhead feeding frenzy comes to a sudden and mysterious halt the moment I arrive? It's not completely original, but it's been a while. Or perhaps something really different, like a plague of flying Gila monsters? Now that would be interesting.

Oh well. It had to be something. Wind that can blow a full-sized truck around doesn't leave much chance for a fly line weighing in at a couple of ounces to straighten out properly. The comforting notion that maybe God wanted me to fish on this day rather than the day before suddenly went cold. The day before the weather had been perfect. I didn't bother spending much time on the idea that it might be less windy at the river. I'm fairly certain that they only settled on the name "Rivière des Chutes" because "Source de Tout Vent" (Source of All Wind) seemed a tad hyperbolic.

I started by hiking quite a way upstream (what was I going to do, turn around and go home again?), above all of the other lunatics (sorry, "devoted anglers") who were out that day. Just before the trail started to get nasty, I found a decent looking run that was unoccupied. The wind was blowing relentlessly. It was going to be difficult just to keep from planting a size 4 hook in my head, much less lay out a nice cast.

"Klaatu… barada… nikto!" I offered, with perhaps a tad less than absolute conviction. Hey, it (usually) works in the movies.

A gust of wind nearly knocked me into the river. Oh well. I think I pronounced it right…

I went to work fishing the run. I was managing to lay my line and leader out nicely, and right where I wanted them; despite the fact that, at least based on the appearance of the amorphous mass of line flopping away from my rod, with no discernable loop whatsoever, I seemed to have completely forgotten how to cast a two-handed fly rod.

It wasn't more than fifteen minutes in that I felt a grab at the end of the swing. It was a good hard tug, and I lifted the rod and felt the fish.

Swinging flies for steelhead is a lot like baseball. I can remember as a kid, standing at the plate watching the pitch coming in and thinking "That's not a strike, don't swing", while my body, apparently no longer under the control of my conscious mind, went ahead and swung anyway, missing the ball by a country mile. Your brain has to convince your hands to stay back until told to do otherwise *ahead* of time. That's 90% of hitting. Swinging flies is the same. Wait, Yogi Berra said that 90% of baseball is half mental, so 45% of baseball is mental. Same with steelheading. My brain said "wait". The fish has to turn in order to get a good hook-set. My hands acted on their own. Stupid hands…

The fish immediately went airborne, gave one good head shake, and was gone. Uuugh.

I stripped the line in to examine the fly. The hook was bent wide open. Huh? It looked like an average fish, maybe six to eight pounds. One head shake? What kind of crappy hook is this? No, that's not it. That was a good quality hook. It sure wasn't because I pulled the trigger too soon. I was baffled.

I passed most of the rest of the afternoon battling the wind (which almost sent me into the river on several occasions), questioning my own sanity, and finding no fish. The Curse seemed to have struck again, and with particular malice.

It was close to the end of the day when I was able to drop in to one of the prime runs. The sun had dipped below the canyon rim, and shadows stretched quickly across the water. The air began to cool, and even the wind finally granted a partial reprieve. In the false dusk of the river canyon a few caddis fluttered about, and here and there a trout rose to snatch one from the surface. Out of the corner of my eye, I saw a large fish roll far out in the river, beyond the reach of a cast. Off in the distance, the northern face of the Columbia Gorge was lit by the late afternoon sun.

Near the end of a long, peaceful swing I felt the grab. First a jolt that ran up the line, through the rod, and into my hands. Then the line coming tight. I lifted the rod and felt a hard pull as the fish turned. It felt powerful and heavy, and was making a run for the middle of the river. My God there are a lot of sunken rocks in this place. Anything could go wrong.

It was pulling hard, but not terribly fast; a bit like being hooked in to a defensive end. Steelhead are usually more like a great running back. There may be stronger men on the field, but they have plenty of power, and combined with explosive speed, they will sometimes go right through a bigger man. They can outrun you if you let them get loose in the open field. They are agile, and changing direction quickly, can leave an opponent crashing to the ground in an attempt to tackle someone who was there a split second earlier. And, just when you think you have your defense set to counter their speed and strength, into the sky they go, leaving you to watch helplessly as they land in the end zone. All of these things, a steelhead is. What I had was something else. Or so it seemed.

The fish broke the surface in the middle of the river. It was at least a hundred feet away, but I could tell it was big. Or at least its tail was big. Like, really freakin' big. I knew there were Chinook in the river, though the technique I was using, swinging a small, sparsely dressed fly on a floating line, is not generally considered the best way to hook one. Still, I'd been told that it happens sometimes.

As the battle went on it became clear what was on the other end of my line. The fish stayed out in the current, maybe thirty feet away, leaning its weight and strength against the rod, using the current, but not draining itself with long runs. It was the (seemingly) endless, bulldogging fight of a Chinook. I didn't have the firepower to horse it in, and the struggle continued for a good twenty minutes. In the end I abandoned the notion of using my steelhead net on the thing, and instead tailed a solid, twenty-pound male Chinook. It was just beginning to show some red on it's flanks, and was in great condition.

Oncorhynchus *tshawytscha*. Looks like someone forgot about a species. Attention to detail indeed…

So, it wasn't what I came for, and I have a habit of getting my heart set on one type of fish when I go out. Steelhead are exempt from that rule, by the way. I could be streamer fishing the salt for Kraken, and I would still be excited about hooking a steelhead. Anyway, I was a little disappointed at the time. I really wanted a steelhead. Only later did I kick myself for not fully appreciating the moment.

I did remember to examine the hook, though. I hadn't forgotten the incident from earlier, which was still puzzling me. I wasn't still fishing the same fly, but it was the same type of hook, and it held up fine against a twenty pound chinook. That steelhead couldn't have straightened the hook… Wait a minute, now I remember. I hung the fly up on a rock a few casts before that first fish took, and had to try every trick in the book before it came loose. It didn't seem like enough to bend the hook, but it must have been. I didn't check it.

Oh, that's a nice touch, really. Bravo. That really adds insult to injury. Give me my one take right after (%##@!=*&!!) up my hook. That's beautiful. Now it's all *my* fault.

I'm sure there are still some out there who would dismiss the existence of fishing curses as superstitious mumbo-jumbo. I know, it's hard to believe. Poor S.O.B.s have probably never known the joys of angling. Then again, it pays to know who you're listening to. The father of a six-year-old girl, for example, could become so over-exposed to Disney Princess-type fairy tales that believing in curses seems perfectly reasonable; just like the perfectly reasonable notion of a smokin' hot French chick who shuns the boorish local alpha-male only to fall in love with the nine-foot-tall werewolf who held her prisoner against her will.

Hey, maybe that's the ticket. I just need to get a hot French girl to fall for me. It worked for the werewolf. Oh, sorry, "The Beast". Whatever. I know a werewolf when I see one. Anyway, it sounds like a lot of trouble. I got a hot German girl to fall for me once. I even convinced her to marry me, but it was no small task. It took Jacob less time to land Rachel. No, I'll just have to keep plugging away. No wait, I mean swinging away.

Maybe I *should* ask Jobu to come. I'm sure I have some rum in the house...